Malbec
mon amour

Malbec mon amour
Laura Catena and Alejandro Vigil

editores

Avenida Donado 4694 - C1430DTP
Buenos Aires, Argentina
info@catapulta.net
www.catapulta.net

Idea & Authorship: Laura Catena and Alejandro Vigil

Editorial team:
General editing: Victoria Blanco
Coordination: Agostina Martínez Márquez
Historical content research: Silvana Baro
Illustrations: Júlia Barata and Martina Trach
Cover design, interior and infographics: Pablo Ayala
Text editing: chapters 1, 2, 3, 4 y 5: Paula Mahler; chapters 6 & 7: Victoria Blanco

First edition.

ISBN 978-987-637-973-1

Printed in China on june 2021.

Catena, Laura
    Malbec Mon Amour / Laura Catena ; Alejandro Vigil. - 1a ed. - Ciudad
Autónoma de Buenos Aires : Catapulta , 2021.
    200 p. ; 28 x 20 cm.

    ISBN 978-987-637-973-1

    1. Vino. 2. Historia. 3. Geografía. I. Vigil, Alejandro. II. Título.
    CDD 641.2223

La presente publicación se ajusta a la representación oficial del territorio de
la República Argentina establecida por el Poder Ejecutivo Nacional a través
del Instituto Geográfico Nacional por Ley N° 22.963 y su impresión ha sido
aprobada por EX-2021-47941977--APN-DNSG#IGN, de fecha 7 de junio de 2021.

LAURA
CATENA

ALEJANDRO
VIGIL

Malbec
mon amour

Catapulta

CONTENTS

THE IMPORTANCE OF TERROIR

ROAD TRIP THROUGH THE UCO VALLEY AND OTHER WINE REGIONS

To the Catena family, especially Dr Nicolás Catena, who is a constant source of inspiration and ideas for my winemaking and that of Argentina as a whole.

And with the deepest recognition to my children and wife, as well as to grandfather Tristán who was always ready to put a roof over my head.

ALEJANDRO VIGIL

To the land of Mendoza
and its inhabitants.

And to the bees, owls, skunks,
insects, plants and microbes
whose generosity allows us
to grow vines year after year.

LAURA CATENA

1

The Romans, Eleanor and the **Malbec Grape**

A BRIEF HISTORY
OF MALBEC

In Argentina, many people think of Malbec as a local variety. And those who know a little more about its history see the grape as an immigrant whose splendid adaptation makes her Argentine through and through. This would be all well and good if it weren't for the fact that Malbec has been so extensively documented in France's wine bibliography. It is impossible to deny the grape's glorious European past.

Malbec's long, eventful history in France is reflected in the number of different names it was given over the years. In the mid 1960s, the French ampelographer Pierre Galet identified more than a thousand different terms for Malbec depending on where it was grown or whomever introduced it to the region in question. For instance, it's known as *Côt* in the Loire Valley, *Malbec* or *Malbec Doux* in Gironde, *Luckens* or *Lutkens* in Médoc, *Pressac* in the Libourne area of Bordeaux, *Côte Rouge* in Entre-deux-Mers and Lot-et-Garonne, and *Auxerrois* or *Côt Noir* in Cahors, capital of the former province of Quercy.

In the 18th and early 19th centuries, Bordeaux clarets were light and almost pink in color, as opposed to their competition, Burgundian Pinot Noir, which was dense, fruity and deeply colored. It is likely that Malbec was a catalyst for the transition of Bordeaux wines into the more concentrated style we know today. These days Pinot Noir is the lighter, paler and more delicate of the two.

Esteemed and respected Professor Vigil,

Following our most recent correspondence, I was left thinking about how wine was preserved in Roman times. The great Cato recommended adding vinegar and sea water to cut the sweetness of grapes that had spent some time drying in the sun. The resulting drink was more water than wine and was kept in amphorae for a year.

Lady Laura Catena y Zapata, your most faithful admirer

DNA ANALYSIS CARRIED OUT IN FRANCE IN 2009 DETERMINED THAT MAGDELEINE NOIRE WAS THE MOTHER OF MALBEC, AND PRUNELARD ITS FATHER.

The former, which also gave birth to Merlot, comes from the Charentes region, about 80 miles north of Bordeaux, while the fruity and tannic Prunelard hails from Gaillac, located between Bordeaux and Cahors. The cross-pollination probably occurred on the banks of the River Lot in Cahors, perhaps before France was conquered by Roman legions or later, in the Middle Ages.

The Malbec Family

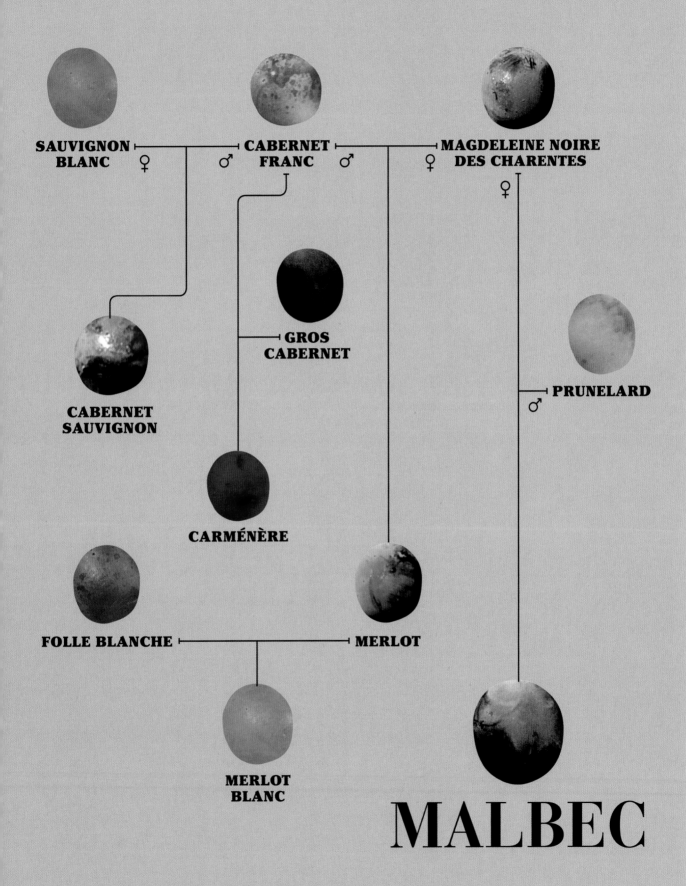

SAUVIGNON BLANC ♀

CABERNET FRANC ♂

MAGDELEINE NOIRE DES CHARENTES ♀

GROS CABERNET

CABERNET SAUVIGNON

PRUNELARD ♂

CARMÉNÈRE

FOLLE BLANCHE

MERLOT

MERLOT BLANC

MALBEC

*Sizes and colors are solely illustrative.

—Lady Laura, my husband the king says he knows more about wine than I do. But I grew up in the vineyards of Aquitaine and I obviously have a more discerning palate than he does... he gets very upset when I tell him so.

—Your Majesty, today we are well aware that women tend to have better palates than men. A study published in *Nature Neuroscience* in 2002 showed that women are up to ten times more sensitive to certain aromas and flavors than men. But don't tell your husband, Your Majesty, he might send you back to prison for a second time.

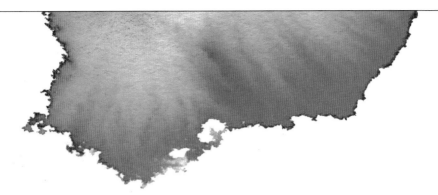

WINEMAKING IS MORE A WAY OF LIFE THAN A JOB. WHAT LAURA AND ELEANOR OF AQUITAINE HAVE IN COMMON IS THEIR LIFELONG COMMITMENT TO GROWING VINES AND MAKING WINE AS A WAY OF LIFE. THEIR PROFOUND LOVE OF WINE, AND SPECIFICALLY MALBEC, HAS GIVEN RISE TO THE GRAPE'S RENAISSANCE AT TWO VERY DIFFERENT MOMENTS IN TIME.

ALEJANDRO VIGIL

Around 150 A.D., the city of Cahors, which was known as Divona at the time, was the Roman capital of the province of Quercy in what is now France. It was here that the first mention of the grape was recorded, although its precise origins continue to be a mystery. Malbec might have come to Divona from Italy, brought by the Roman invaders, or perhaps it was already in France when the Romans arrived in Gaul, and they simply adopted it and continued its cultivation. It is also featured in literary history: praise for the ancient wine of Cahors can be found in the Odes of Horace and in Virgil's poems.

Historians agree that in spite of the foreign invasions that occurred during the decline of the Roman empire, Malbec retained its reputation and continued to be grown.

When we get to the Middle Ages, the story of Malbec becomes inextricably entwined with that of Eleanor of Aquitaine (1122–1204) the only woman ever to be queen of both France and England. Eleanor inherited a third of present-day France, the Duchy of Aquitaine, from her father. Malbec plantations are thought to have extended beyond Cahors down to the Pyrenees (Madiran) in the South and across the eastern bank of the Dordogne River from Saint-Émilion to Côtes de Bourg.

Eleanor preferred the wine from her region over the offerings from the Loire and Burgundy generally chosen by the Parisian aristocracy. At age fifteen, she was married to the man who would soon become Louis VII of France. Later on, the "black wine," as Malbec would come to be known, most likely flowed at Eleanor's Courts of Love, festivals of music and poetry where Malbec grew to be appreciated as the wine of the nobility.

According to oral tradition, the Malbec grape expanded from its native Cahors to Bordeaux in the 18th century, introduced by a Hungarian winemaker called Malbeck or Malbek. In Bordeaux, producers used it to lend more color to their clarets.

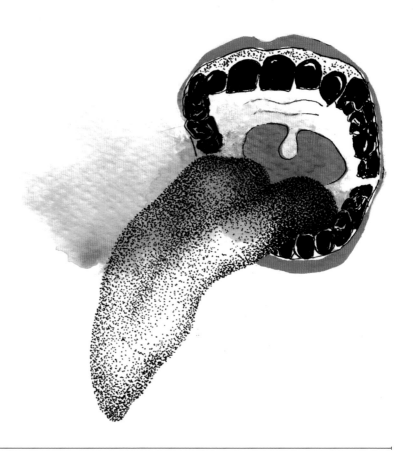

WHY IS MALBEC KNOWN AS "THE BLACK WINE"? THE EXACT ORIGIN OF THE TERM IS UNKNOWN. THE EPITHET COULD BE RELATED TO THE BELIEF THAT HARVESTING THE GRAPES AT NIGHT IMPROVED THE QUALITY OF THE WINE, OR TO THE FACT THAT MALBEC'S INTENSE COLOR LEFT DARK STAINS ON TEETH AND TONGUE.

After fifteen years of marriage, Eleanor divorced Louis VII and renounced the French crown to marry Henry II of England. Their wedding was most likely drenched in Malbec, the royal wine, as chronicled by the era's historians.

The union allowed Aquitaine, now under English rule, to sell the Cahors wines alongside those from Bordeaux across the channel. Malbec now was served at tables across England and Ireland. The children of Henry II and Eleanor who came to the throne, Richard the Lionheart and King John, continued to trade with Cahors and promote the wine.

But an enterprising bureaucrat also played a major role in the growth of wine exports from the Cahors region. In having the boulders removed from the River Lot, which runs through the area, he ensured that circulation and shipping from the interior would be greatly facilitated, much to the benefit of local wine producers. The move also spawned the birth of a rivalry with Bordeaux, whose officials introduced new taxes and restrictions to limit the spread of Malbec from Cahors. To stem this, Henry III of England placed Cahors wine under his personal protection, meaning that Bordeaux officials could not restrict its transport or sale.

Esteemed noblewoman, Lady Laura Catena y Zapata,

In Aquitaine, Malbec was considered the "saviour"
grape because its dark color and rich tannins allowed the
region's *vignerons* to improve, by blending, wines of lesser
concentration. Malbec's reputation and sales continued to
grow, even throughout the Hundred Years War.

Sir Alejandro Vigil,
Thirteenth of February of the year MCDL

English traders soon recognized a good business opportunity at hand, and turned Cahors into a major urban and financial center. The main thoroughfare to foreign markets was the port of La Rochelle, which also flourished as an economic powerhouse. Centuries later, Alexandre Dumas would choose the port as setting for his classic *The Three Musketeers*.

The grape's prestige continued to rise, and by the 16th century, France's Francis I, who was originally from Aquitaine, took such a great liking to Malbec that the grape came to be known as the *Plante du Roi* (the King's Plant). The sovereign planted Malbec around his Palace of Fontainebleau and at his favorite retreat, the Vauluisant Abbey north of Dijon. It was also the dawn of the French Renaissance, and the king's influence made itself felt in the art world. He brought none other than Leonardo da Vinci to his court. It is thanks to Francis I that the *Mona Lisa* hangs today in the Louvre museum.

And let's not forget that the Catholic Church uses wine in its central act of worship: the Mass. History records that when a cobbler's son from Cahors was chosen to be Pope John XXII (1244–1334), he declared Malbec to be the preferred communion wine. When the Pope was living in Avignon during the Schism with Rome, he grew Malbec at his palace. That's not all: By the end of the 17th century, the variety had also become the sacramental wine of the Russian Orthodox Church. Tsar Peter the Great had chosen it as a cure for his stomach ulcers. In fact, Peter had Malbec vines brought from Cahors to Russian Crimea, where it became known as Caorskoie.

Malbec's storied past is marked by historical serendipity, territorial alliances, sacred uses and healthy attributes. Popes, kings, and nameless bureaucrats all had a role in establishing the grape as one of the most important varieties on the European viticultural stage.

My trip to Cahors was a pilgrimage to the original home of Malbec. Today, DNA analyses give us a glimpse into our ancestral origins. Malbec is a part of our family, and I wanted to see the place where the grape was born. In the city of Cahors, there is a center for the promotion and study of Malbec. There, I met the distinguished Professor Laborie, a French expert in the variety, who helped me locate sources on the history of the grape in France. I was also fortunate enough to visit the famous Pont Valentré, which dates back to the 14th century and is a symbol of the city of Cahors, just like the Eiffel Tower is a symbol of Paris.

Laura Catena

But Laura, I wonder: Is place so important? Making wine is more about philosophy and lifestyle. It doesn't really matter where you're making the wine. Making wine is about planting a vineyard and taking care of it. Making wine is about having respect for the yearly cycle, and knowing that each year is going to be different. It's a choice of how to live and experience life. Anyone can make wine but only a few know how to live it: those who are willing to adapt their entire lives to a repeating cycle that never ceases to surprise.

Alejandro Vigil

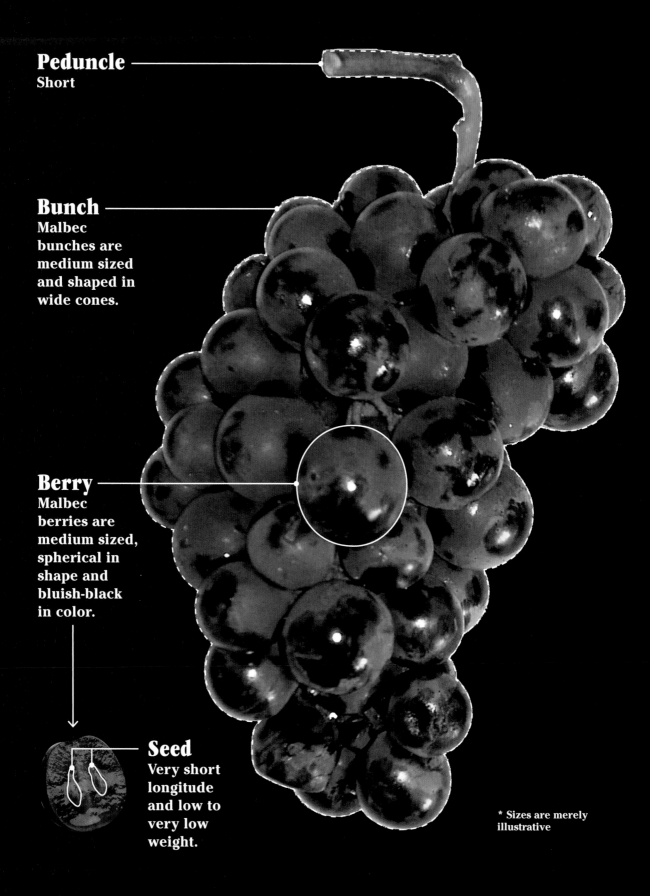

Peduncle
Short

Bunch
Malbec bunches are medium sized and shaped in wide cones.

Berry
Malbec berries are medium sized, spherical in shape and bluish-black in color.

Seed
Very short longitude and low to very low weight.

* Sizes are merely illustrative

1 cm

The Malbec grape is susceptible to shot berries (*coulure* and *millerandage*), especially in difficult climatic conditions such as cold spring weather or high winds during budding season.

Leaves

Adult Malbec leaves are medium sized, polymorphic and mostly whole or having three lobes. Its edges are serrated. The petiole's insertion onto the leaf presents a V or U shape.

Comparison with Cabernet Sauvignon

Main lobe

Lateral lobes

Petiole sinus

Petiole

Tri-lobed leaf

Whole leaf

MALBEC

CABERNET SAUVIGNON

AN AGRICULTURAL TREATISE ON 19TH-CENTURY BORDEAUX VINEYARDS WRITTEN BY AUGUSTE PETIT LAFITTE AND PUBLISHED IN 1868 DESCRIBES MALBEC AS A VARIETY WITH "WINGED AND PYRAMID-SHAPED BUNCHES. THE WINE HAS AN INTENSE COLOR WITH GOOD FLAVOR, RICH AND FIRM".

(Average dates taken from the Colección Chacras de Coria, INTA, Mendoza)

Budding
September 29

Flowering
November 10

Ripening
March 5

Yellowing of the leaves
May 4

same
vinifera
vine
variety

Vinifera root
Vine planted
without grafting
a graft.

Rootstock
About 90% of vines in Argentina are planted on their own *vitis vinifera* roots (ungrafted). Ungrafted Malbec has roots that dig deeply into the soil, sometimes deeper than two meters (six feet), achieving better access to deep water in the soil. Ungrafted vines are able to survive in Argentina because of the low levels of phylloxera and nematodes (tiny worms that attack the vine roots). It is advisable to plant more shallow rooted varieties like Pinot Noir and Chardonnay grafted onto American rootstocks.

Training systems and pruning
Because its shoots tend to rise up straight, Malbec is well suited to a vertical trellis with the upwards positioning seen in the Guyot, Bilateral Cordon, and Lira systems. The classic training system is the vertical trellis with four wires. The total height of the trellis is six feet, and the rows are oriented north to south so as to achieve better sunlight exposure.

MALBEC - GRAFTED

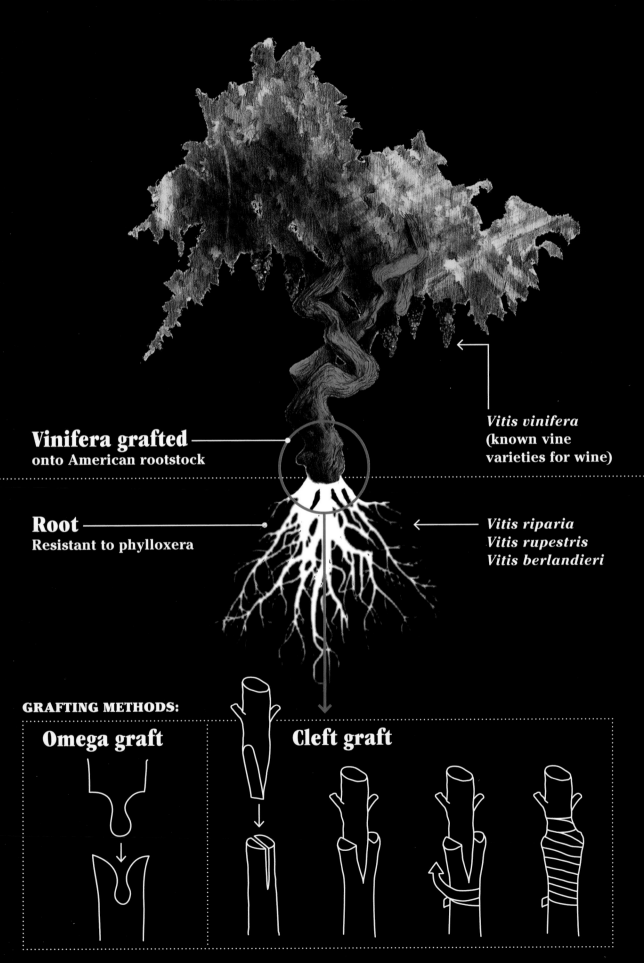

Vinifera grafted
onto American rootstock

Vitis vinifera
**(known vine
varieties for wine)**

Root
Resistant to phylloxera

Vitis riparia
Vitis rupestris
Vitis berlandieri

GRAFTING METHODS:

Omega graft

Cleft graft

2

19th-Century
Aquitaine

FROM THE LAND
OF WINE

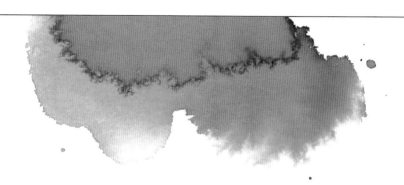

During the three centuries that Aquitaine was governed by the English Crown, consumption of wine from Cahors rose steadily. The defeat of the English in 1453 ended the Hundred Years War and heralded a period of vineyard reconstruction and improved roads, shipping lanes and transport. During the second half of the 17th and throughout the 18th century, the Malbec variety spread farther west throughout the Médoc. In Bordeaux, Malbec became one of the most commonly planted grapes because it added color, aromas and gentle tannins to the celebrated clarets of the area. In 1855, Napoleon III asked the Syndicate of Wine Traders to classify the Bordeaux wines that were to be presented to the world at the Universal Exposition in Paris.

The classification followed two major parameters: the reputation of each chateau and the wine's market price. Reds were cataloged in five rankings: first, second, third, fourth and fifth *grands crus*. Among the Bordeaux Chateaux chosen as *grands crus* in the 1855 Classification, Malbec was the most important variety next to Cabernet Sauvignon.

The Grand Encyclopedia of France, published in 1866, notes: "In the southwest of France, Malbeck, or Côt, is very important; it is part of the make-up of Bordeaux wines and occupies a position of prominence in the Lot region. The wine is of notable quality when the variety is planted in loamy soils and in climates where temperature variations are not too abrupt."

Official classification of 1855 cataloging the best vineyards of Bordeaux (at the time, a large part of these properties were planted with Malbec).

Monsieur Vigil,

Even the luxury of a fabulous chateau is insignificant compared to the music that emanates from the vineyard, representing the cycle of life in all its simplicity. In winter, the twisted vines look like skeletons. In spring and summer, we hear the whispering of leaves rustling in the wind. Birds, insects and glorious flower aromas remind us of why we are alive. We vineyard keepers need that music more than anything else in the world.

Vôtre soeur et amie,

Laura

To prepare for the future we must be cognizant of the past. The study of ancient scientific and non-scientific texts will always help us to improve our present, to understand it and interpret it with an eye on the future. The past opens the door to what lies ahead.

The 1875 edition of the Encyclopedia Britannica agrees: "The main red varieties planted in Médoc are Cabernet Sauvignon, Merlot and Malbec. The most often chosen variety, however, is Malbec, which ripens early; its main disadvantage being its susceptibility to frosts." Other texts from the time confirm that before the phylloxera plague of 1870 devastated most of the vineyards of France and Europe, Malbec plantations represented 60% of the vineyards of Château Cheval Blanc and the Saint-Émilion region. In the early part of the 19th century, Monsieur Lamothe, the administrator of Château Latour, stated that there were two noble varieties planted in the first growth's Médoc property: Malbec and Cabernet Sauvignon. In the treatise on viticulture and oenology published by John Louis William Thudichum and August Dupré in 1829, it is stated: "The Malbec variety prospers in consistent soils but also in gravelly soils so long as they are not too poor in organic matter. It is an early ripening grape with intense flavor and sweetness." Further praise comes from the Count of Odart, a respected oenologist at the time, who advised vineyard owners to add Malbec from Cahors to their Cabernet because it was a structured wine with a vivid dark color, and could even be added to whites to lend greater character. An interesting distinction between Bordeaux Malbec and that grown elsewhere in France appears in a study of the wines of Bordeaux published in 1867 by Armand d'Armailhacq, a Médoc viticulturist.

Armand d'Armailhacq observes that Malbec produces gentle wines with intense flavor and sweetness, tempering the astringency of the Cabernet. He describes it as a less vigorous variety than Cabernet but more productive and delicate in many aspects. After reaching ripeness, he adds, Malbec is prone to rot similarly to Merlot, a variety with which it shares many characteristics. "Malbec is more easily recognized than other varieties due to the vivid red color of its pedicels. The leaves are thicker than those of Cabernet, of a darker shade when fully grown, but whitish with a fine cottony pubescence in the early part of the season. Malbec leaves usually have three rounded lobes with small teeth. The petiole is shorter than that of Cabernet and of a tender green."

He continues: "The most favorable soil for this variety is sandy clay. In alluvial soils it is a very productive grape and often requires a trellis. In gravelly soils Malbec is less productive, and has better flowering when the subsoil is fertile. One must avoid planting it in rocky soils with high iron content as this combination makes the earth sterile. Malbec grows well in sheltered areas and in north and west-facing slopes. In fertile, clay soils, it develops a distinctive taste, of the terroir, but without complexity. Malbec gives rise to different wines depending on the soil and climate where it is grown, as we see in the Malbec of Touraine as compared to the Malbec from Médoc."

I daresay that out of all grape varieties, Malbec has the most interesting history. Which is why I wrote a play about its origins and presented it, fully disguised with costume and wig, at the legendary Nantucket Wine Festival in the USA!

The Malbec plants in Bordeaux were less productive, with smaller berries, than Malbec from other areas. Of note, the first Malbec vines planted in Argentina in 1853 were originally from Bordeaux and therefore presented lower yields, smaller berries, greater concentration and the resulting higher quality. In France, in contrast, after the phylloxera plague only the more productive variety of Malbec survived, called Côt, which tends to be higher yielding with a less delicate flavor.

During the 19th century, agronomists developed the field of ampelography, which focuses on identifying and classifying vines based on individual physical characteristics. In a text about 19th-century grape varieties published in 1841 by the Count of Odart, emphasis is placed on both the variety's ampelographic characteristics—shape of the bunches, berries and leaves, and ripening cycle—and organoleptic qualities—aroma, flavor and color—as the determining factors for wine quality. In that regard, Odart distanced himself from the commonly held view that a vine's behavior was more dependent on climate than on the grape's inborn characteristics—a view based on the writings of the ancient Roman naturalist Pliny.

SCENE FROM THE PLAY ABOUT MALBEC - *PHYLLOXERA*

(Note: She speaks in French with a strong American accent)

Mesdames et messieurs, je suis Phylloxera. Comme ça: Phy-llo-xe-ra.
(She sits on an audience member's lap)

"Bonjour mister, Ça va? Do you like grapes? (offers him some...) I love grapes. I love them so, so much... Ordinarily, I'm a fairly level-headed insect but when I come across a lovely, tasty vineyard, I go a little crazy. And here in France..." (laughs and looks around as though suddenly disoriented)

"Forgive me, do you know where I can find the Grand Chateau du Médoc? (smiles) Or rather, where it was? Ha ha ha ha! It's no longer there, no longer! Because it's now inside my belly! (she laughs as she eats more grapes, food and wine from the guests' tables while rubbing her belly).

"Yes, yes... You know... I'm AMERICAN, a-mer-i-can, and I'm lethal baby, Yeah! Hahahaha."

Odart summarizes his views:

"A FACTOR THAT WOULD APPEAR TO HAVE A MAJOR EFFECT ON THE QUALITY OF A WINE IS THE NATURE OF THE PLANT FROM WHICH IT IS MADE. IT IS WITHOUT A DOUBT THE NATURE OF THE PLANT WHICH DETERMINES THE COLOR, FLAVOR AND SPIRIT OF THE WINE MADE."

Other 19th-century erudites such as Adolphe Magen and Armand d'Armailhacq emphasized the importance of soil. Adolphe Magen based his opinions on the writings of 17th-century agronomist Olivier de Serres, who affirmed that "white" or "cool" soils with calcareous stones lent heat and strength (alcohol content) to the wines. "Dark" or "warm" soils, in contrast, such as clay-based ones, conferred sweetness and refinement. Round, polished rocks lying at the foot of the vines were thought to contribute needed warmth to the vine and clusters, while also preserving moisture under the surface. Olivier de Serres believed that the best soil for viticulture was one made up of gravel and small stones. "This is an irrefutable truth," he wrote: "if one visits the most celebrated vineyards, one will see that the best wines come from calcium carbonate rich soils made up of small stones and fragmented rock."

At the end of the 19th century, the style of Bordeaux wines changed significantly. Following several successive years of cold weather leading to poor set in the Malbec grapes, wine growers in Bordeaux started to favor the cultivation of Cabernet Sauvignon and Merlot, which produced higher and more consistent yields.

THE FINAL BLOW CAME WITH THE PHYLLOXERA PLAGUE, WHICH PRACTICALLY WIPED MALBEC OFF THE MAP. BORDEAUX PRODUCERS DECIDED TO REPLACE IT WITH MERLOT, WHICH RIPENS EARLIER AND IS LESS SUSCEPTIBLE TO POOR SET.

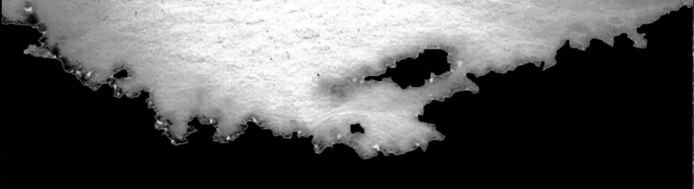

19th-Century Map
European vineyards affected by the phylloxera plague.

Phylloxera Foci

Area invaded in 1880

Area invaded in 1900

Bonn 1874
Worms
Orleans 1875
Maco 1878
Stuttgart
Klosterneuburg 1888
Cognac 1872
Sant Gall 1875
Tokay
Ginebra 1871
Moldavia 1887
Bordeaux 1868
Lecco 1879
Véneto 1920
Budapest
Galicia
Haro 1900
Allold
Oporto 1871
Emilia Romagna 1900
Istria
Serbia 1880
Transilvania 1884
Aranda 1909
Navarra
Gard 1868
Imperia 1879
Girona 1879
Requena 1912
Campania 1920
Bulgaria 1884
Valdepeñas 1911
Tracia
Puglia 1884
Jerez 1894
Málaga 1878
Sicilia 1869
Moreo 1964

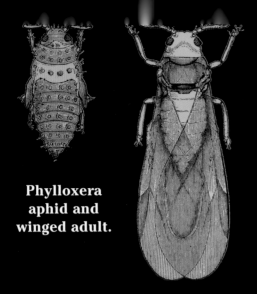

Phylloxera
aphid and
winged adult.

**PHYLLOXERA IS A TINY
APHID, YELLOW IN
COLOR, WHICH ATTACKS
THE LEAVES AND ROOT
FILAMENTS OF THE VINE.
IT MULTIPLIES QUICKLY
AND IS CAPABLE OF
DESTROYING LARGE AREAS
OF VINEYARDS IN A BRIEF
PERIOD OF TIME.**

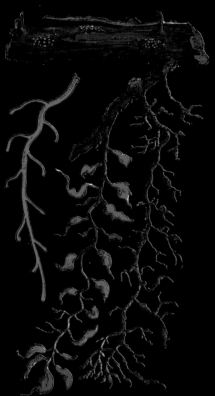

Root infected with phylloxera.

Phylloxera produces galls
on vine leaves.

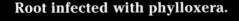

In 1956 a massive frost devastated the Malbec vineyards in Bordeaux and
Cahors. Cahors, the historic cradle of Malbec, continued to grow the grape,
however, where it was blended with other local varieties to make wines
appreciated for their intense color and robust tannins. In 1971 the Cahors
region obtained full AOC, *Appellation d'Origine Contrôlée*, status. The rules
state that for a wine label to carry the Cahors denomination, it must contain
at least 70% Malbec (known in Cahors as *Auxerrois* or *Côt*) and up to 30%
Tannat or Merlot. Today Malbec is still planted in Cahors, Bordeaux and
the Loire Valley, but it is considered a relatively minor variety in France.

3

Puelche, Huarpe and the Pehuenche Peoples,

and how their irrigation canals gave rise to Argentine wine

HOW THE MALBEC GRAPE CAME TO
ARGENTINA

Christopher Columbus is known to have brought cuttings of País and Moscatel from the Canary Islands to America. These vitis vinifera varieties, which could be used to make the sacramental wine, were introduced as part of the Spanish crown's vision of colonization through religious proselytizing. The Spanish vines did not prosper in the Caribbean, but thrived in Mexico, Peru and Chile, where the climate was more temperate and suitable for viticulture.

Midway through the 16th century, Spanish colonists introduced these same varieties, known as "criolla varieties", to Argentina, marking the beginning of Argentine viticulture. Cultivation of criolla varieties became well established and prospered in Mendoza until the middle of the 19th century when new varieties were introduced.

Traveling inland into Mendoza, Argentina, Jesuit missionaries encountered local grapes being grown by the native Huarpe peoples. These autochthonous varieties had a bitter taste, however, and were unsuitable for wine production; the Huarpe used them for dye-making. At the time, vines were planted on terraces and head-trained in the *arbolito* (little tree) system, requiring no wires or posts. Harvest occurred well after the end of summer, in April and May, when the fruit was overripe with a high content of sugars. Grapes were taken to *lagars*, traditional wine presses, in large wicker baskets that were mounted on the backs of mules. The *lagar* press was made of leather. A whole cowhide was split in two to form a large sack in which the grapes were crushed and through which the juice was extracted. The grape juice was collected in buckets, also made of leather, and then poured into large clay containers called *tinajas* where fermentation occurred.

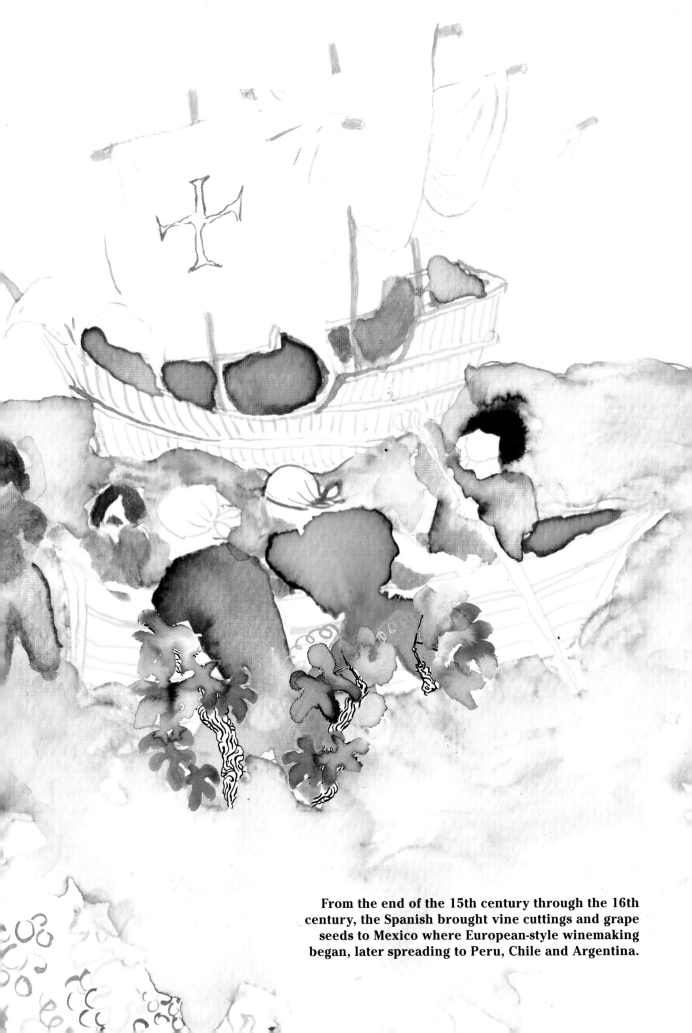

From the end of the 15th century through the 16th century, the Spanish brought vine cuttings and grape seeds to Mexico where European-style winemaking began, later spreading to Peru, Chile and Argentina.

The Huarpe irrigation canals gave rise to Mendoza's water system.

Once fermentation was complete, the wine was strained and then returned once more to clay *tinajas* that were buried under the ground to maintain a low storage temperature. The *tinajas* were then transported by mule or cart, protected by mats of woven reeds or waterproof leather. To ensure the wine's preservation during long journeys, a proportion of cooked grape must was added to the wine in the *tinajas*.

None of this would have been possible if not for the famous Huarpe irrigation system, an essential piece in the development of Mendoza's viticulture.

After their lands were incorporated into the Inca Empire around 1450, the Huarpe peoples applied Inca know-how to create a sophisticated irrigation system that diverted snowmelt from the Andes to part of what is now Greater Mendoza. In his book, "The Vineyard at the End of the World," the American journalist Ian Mount writes about how the Incan emperor "had sent engineers to the valley of Huentata, as Mendoza was then known, to build a gravity-fed irrigation system. The canals they built channeled water from mountain rivers to the valley, where the water was shunted into a series of branches and then to a web of capillary-like ditches that ran beside each arable field. It was a circulatory system with the Andes as its heart...." The irrigated regions encompassed a large part of the current departments of Luján de Cuyo, Godoy Cruz and Guaymallén and part of what is now the town of Las Heras.

CONSEQUENTLY, AS THE HISTORIAN FELIPE PIGNA WRITES: "THE CONQUISTADORS WERE ABLE TO SIMPLY USE THE EXISTING IRRIGATION SYSTEM, WHICH THEY THEN EXPANDED AS THEY SPREAD OUT TO NEW LANDS.

In 1566 the Mendoza government passed an ordinance that required residents with farms bordering the principal irrigation canals to keep the said canals cleaned and in good condition so as to avoid water shortages and flooding due to blockages. The fine for not maintaining one's local canal in good condition was quite high, and could amount to the whole value of a farm."

The church would become an important producer of wine during the colonial period in Argentina, when it was given a sort of monopoly over winemaking by the Spanish king. Argentine historian Pablo Lacoste explains how, in 1595, Phillip II of Spain issued a decree forbidding the planting of vines in the Americas to ensure that Spain's powerful wine producers would have no competition from the New World. Lacoste writes: "An express exception was made for religious orders. However, they were forbidden from exporting their wine to Mexico, which was a market that Spanish producers wanted to keep for themselves. The result was predictable and almost immediate: the largest wine producing establishments ended up in the hands of priests and monks." Religious orders invested in developing vineyards and wineries, building money-making enterprises that helped finance missionary activities.

There are those who challenge this version of events, arguing that the prohibition was not followed in practice. Clarence H. Haring proposed in his 1947 paper, "The Spanish Empire in America," that the wine industry in colonial territories such as Chile and Mendoza (in present-day Argentina), whose climate and soil were well suited to viticulture, flourished in spite of Cadiz' best efforts to enforce a Spanish wine monopoly. In the end, it would appear that the local South American producers gave up any pretense at obeying the law. There is no doubt that viticulture in Cuyo continued to grow and in practice supplied enough wine to meet the demand of the future viceroyalty. This would have been impossible had vines been destroyed and the planting of new ones banned.

The church continued to have a major influence on the wine industry until the end of the 18th century, when the Jesuits were expelled from the viceroyalty. Jesuit priests had been talented winemakers. They used the most modern and effective equipment available such as brick and lime vats, as opposed to the less hygienic leather containers. Because the other Catholic orders and the secular clergy did not have the know-how to replace the Jesuits, the church's influence on wine production declined.

Meanwhile, the local population embraced winemaking with increased freedom after independence from Spain. Argentina's revolutionary hero, General José de San Martín, also known as the liberator of Chile, Argentina and Peru, played a role in the development of Argentina's post-colonial wine industry.

General, we have you to thank for Mendoza becoming the grand center of Argentine wine.

According to Mendoza historian Ricardo Videla, General San Martín, a fine wine lover, helped to establish the Cuyo wine industry. Videla observes that in spite of the general's many duties as head of the Andean Army, he was curious about farming and winemaking technologies and often toured the vineyards of Mendoza.

Argentine historian Felipe Pigna tells a well-known anecdote about San Martín that highlights the general's affinity for Argentine wine. One day, while the training of the army was in progress, General San Martín summoned Manuel de Olazábal, a young lieutenant and hardened soldier, to share a secret about a wine tasting that he was planning for the evening.

Olazábal would tell in his memoirs that San Martín had organized a blind tasting for a group of officers he'd invited to dinner. He planned to serve them a Mendoza wine in a bottle dressed with a Spanish Málaga label and a Spanish wine in a bottle dressed with a Mendoza label. "Today for dessert, I shall have the bottles brought over and we shall see what kind of Americans we are, always preferring goods from overseas," San Martín had said to Olazábal. After the meal, San Martín asked for the wines to be poured and addressed his guests: "Let's see which you think is best." He served the Málaga wine labeled 'Mendoza' first. The guests declared that it was a good wine but lacked fragrance. Then the glasses were filled with wine marked 'Málaga' but which was actually from Mendoza. The officers immediately burst out with: "Oh, there's a big difference!

My dear esteemed lady,
I have chosen wine as a source
of sustenance and energy for
my brave soldiers who crossed
the Andes and fought the decisive
battles against the Spaniards
in Chile.

Many thought it would be impossible to cross the Andes with an army of 5,000 men. Perhaps we have the General's meticulous planning to thank for this improbable feat. And perhaps wine played an important role in San Martin's strategy: he assigned 113 mules to transport wine for the troops, ensuring a bottle per day for each soldier.

This is exquisite, there's no comparison..." The general broke down in laughter and chastised the officers, saying: "Gentlemen, you know nothing about wine, and you are blinded by foreign labels." He then told them the trick he'd played on them.

This story is told by many historians and chroniclers of the times. Indeed, San Martín was a genuine wine lover who also cultivated a small vineyard in Mendoza at his Barriales farm, and later, during his exile in France the general is known to have associated with several important French wine producers.

Let's now turn to the Malbec era, which begins in the middle of the 19th century with an important character, President Domingo Faustino Sarmiento, who is known

as the father of education in Argentina for making public education compulsory and free throughout the Nation. This son of the winemaking region of Cuyo (which includes Mendoza, San Luis and San Juan), born in the Province of San Juan, admired the cultures of France and Britain. At the time, the French were considered the undisputed leaders of quality wines, and in 1853 Sarmiento hired French agronomist Michel Aimé Pouget to create a vine nursery in Mendoza: the Quinta Normal de Agricultura. Pouget brought with him a large shipment of French vines. The grape varieties included Cabernet Sauvignon, Semillon, Chardonnay, Riesling and the first Malbec vines. It was Sarmiento who introduced modern viticultural and winemaking techniques to Argentina.

MEANWHILE, IN EUROPE, AT THE 1855 UNIVERSAL EXPOSITION IN PARIS, A SYSTEM WAS ESTABLISHED TO CLASSIFY THE BEST WINES OF BORDEAUX. AS WE MENTIONED EARLIER, MALBEC MADE UP A SIGNIFICANT PORTION OF THE GRAND CRU RATED WINES.

The most successful wines received the title of *premier grand cru classé*. Lafite Rothschild, Haut-Brion, Latour and Margaux won the highest rating. If the ultimate goal was to set up a high-quality wine industry in Argentina like the one in France, then it made sense to follow Bordeaux's lead by planting Malbec and other varieties from the region.

4

An Industry
Is Born

A TRAIN, A PEOPLE

Michel Aimé Pouget's 1853 arrival in Mendoza marked the entrance of Malbec on the Argentine wine stage. From that moment on, work started on improving Malbec's adaptation to Mendoza's soil and climate. "It was a slow and quiet process which had the local *vigneron* as its protagonist," explains Pablo Lacoste. "The locals applied the experience gained over three centuries to the cultivation of Malbec. And by the time that the railway arrived in Mendoza, in 1885, and European immigrants started to flood into the province in the early 20th century, Malbec was fully adapted to Mendoza."

Plagued by difficulties and limited resources, however, Pouget's official mission, to create a vine nursery, eventually failed. Why? Because the 48 hectares the government had assigned it were arid and rocky, and Pouget was not given the funds and staff necessary to develop them properly. The environment in Mendoza was challenging in general, with a paucity of trees, poor infrastructure and frequent flooding from the disrepair of the irrigation canals. Within two years, Pouget's Quinta Agronómica had suffered through a drought, a flood and a locust infestation. After legislators reduced his salary, Pouget resigned. But he had made his mark on the local wine industry. And in spite of all the setbacks, Pouget stayed in Mendoza and continued to support the region's viticulturists until his death in 1875.

Malbec first came to Argentina in 1853, brought over by the French agronomist Michel Aimé Pouget, who was hired by Domingo Faustino Sarmiento to run the Quinta Normal de Mendoza.

THE BUILDING OF THE RAILWAY THAT CONNECTED MENDOZA TO BUENOS AIRES WAS KEY TO THE MASSIVE EXPANSION OF ARGENTINA'S WINE INDUSTRY.

Previously, horse-led carts had been used to transport wine. The railway allowed wine to be distributed across Argentina and even exported elsewhere—it took the Argentine wine industry to another level.

After leaving the Quinta, Pouget led the transformation of rustic local wines from sweet to elegant. He developed his own land using quality grape varieties newly imported from Europe, such as Cabernet Sauvignon, Merlot, Semillon and Malbec. Pouget was also instrumental in developing modern agricultural techniques, teaching pruning and grafting methods, and introducing the first honeybees to Mendoza. "Pouget founded the first model *bodega* in Argentina and taught vintners winemaking tricks such as using sulfur to conserve wines for long voyages," writes Ian Mount in his book about the rebirth of Malbec in Argentina.

Rail would be the decisive factor in the expansion of Mendozan wine beyond its provincial borders. Inaugurating the railway in 1885, President Julio Argentino Roca made it possible for local wine products to reach Buenos Aires and Santa Fe. Felipe Pigna illustrates the phenomenal importance of the railway with the following statistic: "The journey from Buenos Aires to Mendoza was shortened from two months, the minimum amount of time it took the mule-drawn carriages, to two days, with the new Andino train service." The railway also had an impact on location; wineries built their facilities close to the rails to facilitate loading and unloading. The train brought the first filters, presses, hand pumps and grape crushers. It brought the first wooden casks and barrels, which would eventually replace traditional clay tinajas. Although transportation had taken a massive step forward, the issue of drought remained. Nowadays, only 300,000 hectares, about 3% of the total surface area of Mendoza, has access to irrigation water. In 1896, the situation was even worse.

Up until the 1950s, grapes were pressed by hand in manual presses that required a great deal of effort to operate. To this day, some Argentine wineries still use this traditional method.

Only 33,000 hectares of land had access to irrigation at that time in Mendoza. Water was accessed through a complex system of canals derived from the original Huarpe design. In 1888, the governor of Mendoza, Don Tiburcio Benegas, decided to hire an Italian engineer, Cesare Cipolletti, to implement a revolutionary irrigation project. Cipolletti, who had been orphaned at age seven, was an experienced civil engineer. Cipolletti had worked on the construction of aqueducts in several Italian cities, in the modernization of Swiss irrigation canals, and on water distribution networks in Egypt's northern Nile.. His engineering works enabled the addition of 131,500 hectares of farmland to the province with the construction of the Luján Dam across the Mendoza River and the Medrano Dam across the Tunuyán River. Cipolletti was also responsible for installing the first pipes to supply drinking water in the provinces of Mendoza, San Juan, San Luis and Tucumán, and for helping solve Patagonia's Río Negro flooding in the Alto Valle.

The late 19th century brought major urban development to Mendoza under the governorship of conservative politician Emilio Civit. He was twice Governor of Mendoza and also National Minister of Public Works and Agriculture during the second Roca administration. Civit got so much done that at the end of his term in 1904, Argentine President Roca declared: "In his six years running the ministry, Civit has undertaken such a considerable number of public works as to represent the work of a generation rather than that of a legislative period." Wide open to new ideas, Emilio Civit hired experts such as the architect and landscaper Carlos Thays, the mathematician and statistician Francisco Latzina and the prestigious Argentine physician Emilio Coni to direct his public works.

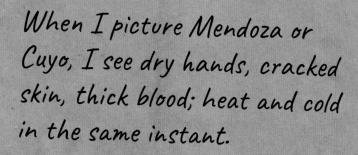

When I picture Mendoza or Cuyo, I see dry hands, cracked skin, thick blood; heat and cold in the same instant.

Our people are one with the mountains and the desert; we are tough and strong, but also tethered by emotion; and blood flows warmly through our veins.

Alejandro

TO THIS DAY, EMILIO CIVIT'S MARK ON MENDOZA IS CLEARLY VISIBLE: ROADS, BRIDGES, IRRIGATION WORKS, ELECTRIC TRAMS, PUBLIC BUILDINGS AND SCHOOLS CARRY HIS SIGNATURE.

Emilio Civit expanded the provincial capital, opened General San Martín Park and built the monument to the Army of the Andes on the Cerro de la Gloria. Less well-known is his influence on the man who would become his father-in-law, governor and vintner Tiburcio Benegas. Civit wrote to Benegas from France with tales about majestic Bordeaux chateaux and meticulously tended vineyards, insisting that Argentine viticulture needed to be modernized.

As author Ian Mount writes:"What moved Civit to write to Benegas with such urgency was not just wide-eyed progressivism, but rather visions of economic opportunity. Civit saw wine for what it was: an increasingly globalized product in which France held price and quality advantages. But, Civit realized, Argentine *bodegueros* were about to have a unique opportunity to steal a piece of the market. As Civit traveled through France, a vine blight was

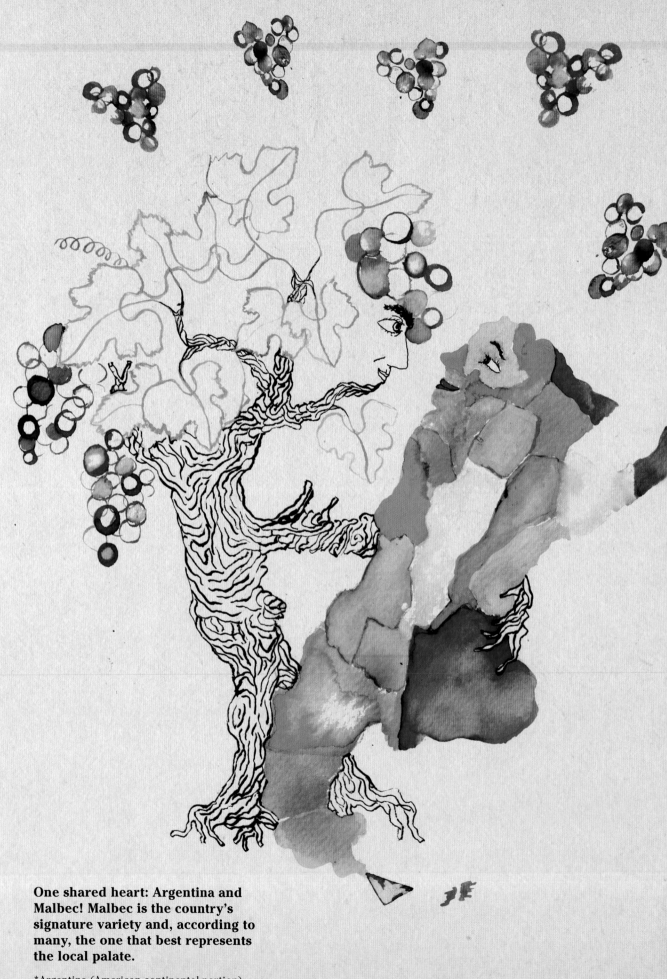

One shared heart: Argentina and Malbec! Malbec is the country's signature variety and, according to many, the one that best represents the local palate.

*Argentina (American continental portion)

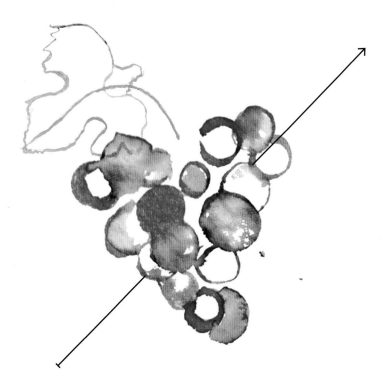

sweeping the country (phylloxera). The supply of European wine was about to fall dramatically, Civit saw, which meant that less imported wine would flow into Argentina's capital city. If Argentina put together a nucleus of capable growers and winemakers schooled in Médoc's best practices, Civit told Benegas, the country could 'completely close the markets of Buenos Aires not only to Bordeaux, but to Italy and Spain as well'."

All this economic and entrepreneurial expansion occurred in a context of very promising times for Argentina at the end of the 19th and beginning of the 20th centuries. The Argentine leadership sought to turn a country blessed with natural resources into one of the world's greatest nations. Buenos Aires showed a marked influence from French architecture, with beautiful buildings that evoked a similar period in Paris. And in Mendoza, even today, one can see the legacy of classic French techniques in the tightly spaced rows of vines and the low and close-to-the-ground vines in some

of Argentina's oldest vineyards.

On the other side of the Atlantic, in France, the Malbec grape, until then a major component of the best Bordeaux blends, the *Premiers Grands Crus Classés*, was being decimated by the phylloxera epidemic. Between 1875 and 1889, the disease led to the demise of around 2,500,000 hectares of vineyards in France.

Meanwhile, back in Argentina, Malbec was adapting marvelously to the soil and climate of Mendoza and gradually becoming the leading grape on the Argentine viticultural scene. By the start of the 20th century, most of the vineyards in Mendoza had been planted with the so-called *uva francesa*, or French grape, the local name given to Malbec. At the same time, the few Malbec vines that survived in France were not adapting well to the American rootstocks brought over to save the European vines from the plague. Because American rootstocks are more vigorous than the native Malbec, the grafted vines developed excessive foliage

and the grapes didn't ripen in time for the harvest—a major disadvantage in France, where rain and cold often forced early pickings.

In addition to the grafting difficulties, Malbec's propensity to shot berries made it more difficult to grow in Bordeaux, where the sometimes cold and rainy weather could stunt the development of the grapes and cause dramatic yield reductions. When the great frost of 1956 decimated Malbec vineyards in Bordeaux and Cahors, they were replaced this time not by Malbec but Cabernet Sauvignon and Merlot grapes. Meanwhile, in Argentina, the pre-phylloxera Malbec vines introduced by Sarmiento prospered in Mendoza at the hands of Italian and Spanish immigrants. The dry climate and alluvial soils in the province restricted the spread of phylloxera to such a degree that the Malbec vines were rarely affected. The mild, dry climate of Mendoza also made Malbec far less prone to shot berries than in Bordeaux. No wonder it is

often said that Malbec and Argentina are a match made in heaven.

And this is how Malbec became yet another successful European immigrant to Argentina. The grape ripened splendidly in Mendoza, where the growing season is long and the desert air is dry. In 1962, a century after Pouget's arrival, the most planted fine red variety in Argentina was Malbec, with 58,577 hectares under vine, 22.5% of the total in the country.

We might ask ourselves: Which is the Old World for Malbec? The ancient populations of Malbec nearly disappeared from Europe after phylloxera, but those that came to Argentina before the plague survived in all their glorious diversity. It would not be wrong then to suggest that today Argentina represents the Old World for Malbec. Yet Argentina's markedly different *terroir*—dry, sunny and high in the mountains—is undeniably New World, and it is the place where Malbec has found its definitive home.

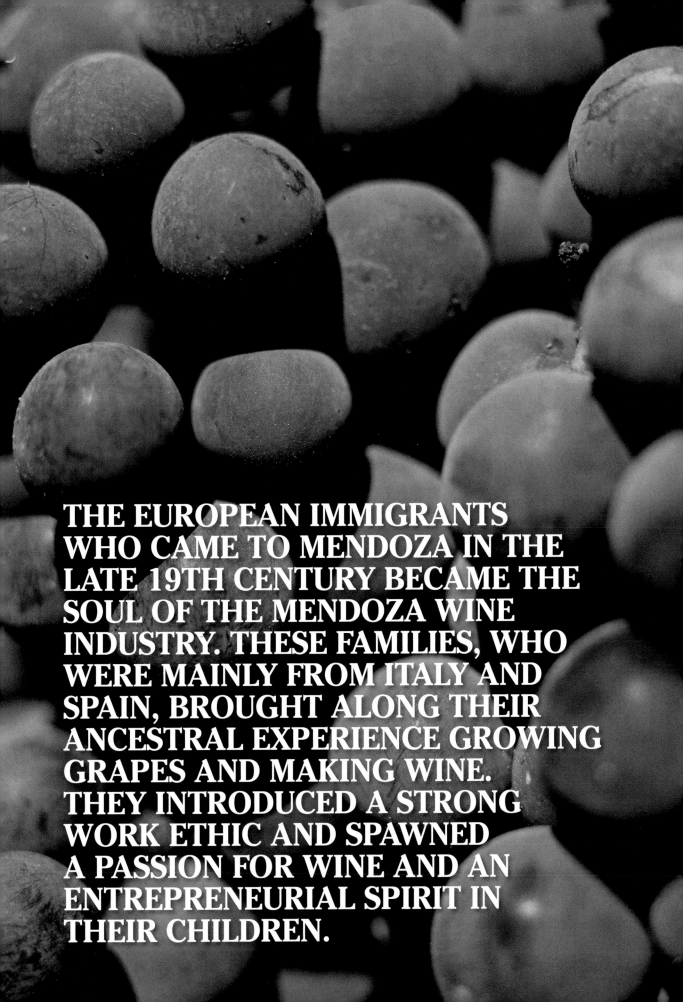

THE EUROPEAN IMMIGRANTS
WHO CAME TO MENDOZA IN THE
LATE 19TH CENTURY BECAME THE
SOUL OF THE MENDOZA WINE
INDUSTRY. THESE FAMILIES, WHO
WERE MAINLY FROM ITALY AND
SPAIN, BROUGHT ALONG THEIR
ANCESTRAL EXPERIENCE GROWING
GRAPES AND MAKING WINE.
THEY INTRODUCED A STRONG
WORK ETHIC AND SPAWNED
A PASSION FOR WINE AND AN
ENTREPRENEURIAL SPIRIT IN
THEIR CHILDREN.

At the age of 18, Nicola Catena arrived in Argentina from Le Marche and settled in Santa Fe Province, where he was welcomed by a family friendly with the Catenas in Italy. Decades later, when the Catenas settled in Mendoza, Domingo, Nicola's son, continued to send a truck full of fruit, ham and wines in gratitude to the family who had hosted his father upon his arrival in Argentina.

NICOLA CATENA EMIGRATED TO ARGENTINA AT THE END OF THE 19TH CENTURY. HE WAS ONE OF THE FIRST WINEMAKERS IN EASTERN MENDOZA AND FOUNDER OF ONE OF THE OLDEST AND MOST PRESTIGIOUS WINERIES IN THE COUNTRY. BORN IN ITALY, IN BELFORTE DEL CHIENTI, A SMALL TOWN IN LE MARCHE REGION, HE FIRST SET FOOT ON ARGENTINE SOIL IN 1898.

Important early figures in the Mendoza wine industry include Carlos González Videla, Segundo Correas, Tiburcio Benegas, Francisco Gabrielli, Balbino Arizu, Lorenzo Vicchi, Antonio Tomba, Pascual Toso, Nicola Catena, Bautista Gargantini, Juan Giol, Miguel Escorihuela Gascón, Felipe Rutini, José Federico López, Ángel Furlotti, Antonio Pulenta, José Orfila and Valentín Bianchi, among others.

Nicola Catena was one of the many 19th-century immigrants to Argentina. As the son of a winemaking family, he learned from a young age each of the tasks involved in cultivating the vine, and always remembered the farming advice given to him by his father, Domenico, and his grandfather Vincenzo. News from Argentina, a land of opportunity, had reached Nicola's small Italian village; the fearless youth, at only 18, decided to undertake the voyage to the New World. Following his arrival in Buenos Aires, Nicola headed to the town of Peyrano in the Province of Santa Fe, home to Italian friends of his parents who had emigrated years before. He was welcomed with extraordinary warmth, embraced as a son and invited to work along with them growing corn. But Nicola's passion had always been wine. He liked to say that he had one, and only one, childhood dream, and that was to one day make his own wine from his own vineyard. And this is how in 1902 Nicola decided to travel to Mendoza, the most important wine-producing region in Argentina. There he bought a 10-hectare property on the banks of the River Tunuyán, in the Department of Rivadavia. According to his grandson Nicolás, Nicola paid for the land with the money given to him by his parents when he set sail for the Americas. Two hectares of the property already contained Malbec vines, and that same year, he was able to plant, with his own hands, two more hectares of Malbec.

Mendoza is currently Latin America's wine powerhouse, and the fifth-largest wine producer in the world with 140,000 hectares (346,000 acres) under vine and hundreds of wineries, many of them exporting their wines around the world.

Nicola built a small house on his land and planted more vines, experimenting with different training methods—low vine, pergola, greater and lesser distance between plants—and different harvest moments. In 1909, he married Anna Moscetta, also originally from Le Marche. They had six children; the eldest, Domingo Vicente, was born in 1910 and succeeded Nicola as leader of the family winery. Nicola's dream had come to fruition: He had made his own wine with his own brands, Catena and La Marchigiana, which he sold in 150-liter barrels to different bottlers in other provinces. He had raised a family that retained the strong work ethic and frugal ways of his ancestors. His children say that Nicola never had any desire to return to Italy, but that when his parents had reached the age of retirement, he invited them to come to Argentina to live with him. Nicola's parents lived their final days under the care of their youngest son in sunny Mendoza.

In 1932, Nicola Catena decided to hand over the running of the family winery to his son Domingo, although he and his wife, Anna, continued to lend their support and help in caring for the family's vineyards. In the early '60s, Domingo became a sort of *négociant* for wine blends out of Mendoza province. He developed the art of blending wines from different areas of Cuyo, including wine from older vintages to increase complexity. Domingo became known around Argentina as the master blender from Mendoza, and his favorite pastime was coming up with new blends. He made sure he always had the last word regarding any wine or barrel sold by his winery. Those familiar with Domingo's skill say that he was capable of discerning the makeup of a wine and its chemistry better than any lab technician.

Nicola Catena and his son Domingo Vicente sent wine in barrels to Buenos Aires. The wines were then bottled in the capital and served at restaurants and steakhouses across the city.

Don Domingo had a clear preference for the flavor of Malbec, while his father Nicola's favorite variety was Bonarda. At lunchtime, the family made sure to put a bottle of each on the table when they came to dine. Grandson Nicolás remembers the two having passionate arguments over what were obviously two very different flavors.

Domingo generally traveled to Europe every year on month-long journeys with the single purpose of tasting wines. He visited Spain, Italy, France and Germany, developing an exceptional palate that allowed him to determine the origins of different wines with remarkable ease. In spite of his Italian heritage, Don Domingo

Anna, Amalia, Emilio, Domingo, Elena, María and Nicola Catena at their home in La Libertad, Rivadavia, Mendoza, Argentina. c. 1920

P. 66: Angélica Zapata and Domingo Vicente Catena, the parents of Nicolás Catena Zapata, at Cerro de la Gloria (c. 1934). The wall seen in the photograph is made of the same stone as La Pirámide, the family winery.

always gave first place in his tastings to the French wines, especially those of Bordeaux; for the whites he favored German Riesling. Domingo's dedication to developing his palate is what undoubtedly helped him become the artist behind some of the most relevant blends to come out Argentina in the 1950s and 1960s. Although he always returned from Europe with genuine admiration for its most famous wines, his vintner friends say that he never stopped proclaiming his ardor for Argentine Malbec, its aroma and flavor. In addition to running the family winery, Don Domingo had a very active political life. He was the head of his party in the Department of Rivadavia and a representative in the legislature of the province of Mendoza. His action-oriented political involvement allowed him to monitor governmental intervention in the wine industry: for many decades Domingo worked to oppose any legislation unfavorable to the wine industry, which he

saw as key to the province's economic welfare. Don Domingo is remembered in Mendoza today for his opinions and participation in the drawing of laws and regulations related to winemaking and viticulture.

In 1934, Don Domingo married Angélica Zapata, and they had four children: Silvia, Nicolás, Jorge and Maria Angélica. The couple passed down not just the immigrant work ethic but also a deep respect for intellectual pursuits, in the hands of the tenacious Angélica. It is said that in her teaching work, Angélica regarded herself as a teacher in the tradition of Sarmiento, which meant dedicating oneself fully to the office regardless of remuneration or the sacrifices required. In her hometown, she is remembered as a school headmistress who never missed a class, a tireless, generous woman who welcomed students in need of extra help at home every day, including on the weekends, so they wouldn't fall behind.

5

Nicolás Catena's
Revolution

WINE AS
A WAY
OF LIFE

Nicolás, son of Domingo and grandson of Nicola, grew up in the vineyards, where he spent the afternoons after school. The family was guided by the life philosophy of most 20th-century immigrants: Improving one's finances required hard work and saving. Nicolás started helping his father and grandfather from the age of six, learning how to perform every task in the vineyard and winery. He was thus introduced from a young age to the land from which he would make wonderful future wines.

"You're too smart to go into business," his mother Angélica would tell him when she saw him head out to the winery after he got back from school. "And if you decide to study science, which seems to be your passion, you should aspire to the Nobel Prize," she added with emphasis. In July 1955, Nicolás had already decided that when he finished secondary school (the Military School attended by the majority of rural children), he would study Physics at the University of Buenos Aires. After all, Bernardo Houssay, who won the Nobel Prize for Medicine in 1947, had studied there. Angélica's prioritizing of the sciences and of intellectual pursuits was rare among rural Italian families. It was generally assumed that Nicolás would continue the family's winemaking tradition like his ancestors had, going all the way back to Italy. However, a tragic event sealed his fate forever. In 1957, his mother, Angélica, and grandfather Nicola were killed in a car accident, rammed head-on by a harvest truck. Nicolás' plans were completely upended.

Released in 1968, the first label of Catena Zapata's Saint Felicien line (1963 vintage) was illustrated with the painting Vendimia, by Mendoza artist Carlos Alonso. Ever since, Saint Felicien has been closely associated with artists and their world.

Goodbye, Buenos Aires. Nicolás decided to stay in Mendoza. He saw no choice. He would study Economic Sciences at the National University of Cuyo, help out his father at the winery and take care of his siblings with his grandmother Nicasia, Angélica's mother.

In 1965, Nicolás took a leadership role in the family winery. The first thing he suggested to his father was that they move from growing and blending to also bottling and selling their own wines. The Catenas bought the Crespi bottling plant in the City of Buenos Aires and a majority stake in Bodegas Esmeralda, which was primarily dedicated to fine wine. In 1968, father and son launched a high-end Cabernet Sauvignon under the Saint Felicien name. It became an instant success. The wraparound label, illustrated with a lithograph inspired by the harvest, had been specially created for this wine by the renowned Mendoza artist Carlos Alonso. To this day, Saint Felicien, the first varietal-labeled wine conceived by Nicolás Catena in the '60s, continues to be one of the most emblematic and traditional fine wine brands in Argentina.

The success of the wine was followed shortly by a financial crisis, which led to massive demand for less expensive wines and a boom in whites and rosés. The result was that thousands of hectares of Malbec were pulled out and the total surface area under vine reduced to about 14,000 hectares. In its place was planted high-yield criolla varieties. Within two decades, Malbec cultivation had been reduced by 80%.

Which is why, by the end of the 1970s, most Argentine wines were characterized by somewhat oxidized aromas, a soft mouthfeel, low aromatic intensity and little varietal typicity.

Dr. Nicolás Catena tasting wine with Robert Mondavi, the father of California wine.

The Judgment of Paris of 1976 was a historic tasting organized by Steven Spurrier, the legendary British wine writer, in which a group of European wine specialists blind tasting French and California wines chose Californian wines as the winners.

Argentine winemaking techniques followed ancient Italian traditions brought over by the immigrants. After three or four years of aging in large, decade-old oak casks, the wines were characterized as smooth and easy on the palate, but the aromas were subdued and the colors rather dull. Soon, however, thanks to the determination of one producer, a major change would take place in the Argentine wine industry. In the 1980s, winemaker and economist Nicolás Catena Zapata started a revolution. He had been invited to the University of California at Berkeley as a visiting scholar. That stay inspired Nicolás to make radical changes to his viticultural and winemaking methods back home. In California's Napa Valley, Catena had the opportunity to taste wines from top California wineries. These wines impressed him with their freshness, fruit and notes of new French oak. In fact, California vintners were on a mission to produce wines that were just as good as—or better than—those from France: Cabernet Sauvignons that could compete with those from Bordeaux, Chardonnays at the level of Burgundy's best whites. Californians believed at the time that adopting French winemaking techniques for classic varieties such as Cabernet Sauvignon would result in a Californian *Grand Cru Classé*. Terroir took a back seat—what mattered was winemaking. A major landmark in this process was the so-called Judgment of Paris, a blind tasting of Californian and French wines organized by the British wine critic Steven Spurrier and held in Paris on May 24, 1976.

Spurrier gathered a group of

The Judgment of Paris was without a doubt the event that began the change in perception of New World wines.

distinguished experts to taste some of the best Chardonnays and Cabernet Sauvignons from California alongside some of the most celebrated Chardonnays from Burgundy and four Cabernet Sauvignon blends designated Bordeaux *Premiers* and *Deuxième Grands Crus*. The participants were stunned by the results: among the whites the winner was Château Montelena Chardonnay from the Napa Valley in California, and among the reds it was Stag's Leap Wine Cellars Cabernet Sauvignon, also from California. For centuries France had regarded itself as the undisputed champion of quality wines, and the famous tasting, its coverage in the press and the resulting market changes were a wake-up call for French producers. Now the New World had emerged as a legitimate competitor, one determined to match France's excellence in wine.

In 1984, upon his return to Argentina, Nicolás Catena asked himself: *If the Americans can aspire to compete with the best European wines, why not me in Argentina?* He got to work, planting selections of the highest-quality Cabernet and Chardonnay clones available in France and the USA in the best micro-climates of Mendoza's traditional winemaking regions. He modernized the family winery, investing in stainless steel tanks so as to carefully monitor fermentation temperatures, and replacing the old wooden casks with new French oak barrels. Later, he hired the California wine consultant Paul Hobbs to help equip the winery with the latest technology.

Alejandro, I'm calling to chat about the famous 1976 Judgment of Paris.

Laura Catena: *Aló*, Alejandro? I'm calling to chat about the 1976 Judgment of Paris.

Alejandro Vigil: The Judgment of Paris, regardless of all the hype that came after, was all about the idea that great wines could be produced outside of Bordeaux or Burgundy; it opened the door not just to the wines involved in the tasting but also for the rest of us.

LC: Like Château Montelena and Stag's Leap.

AV: Right, like Stag's Leap, which is one of my favorite wines... A really incredible Cabernet.

LC: I was invited a while back to a ceremony where The Smithsonian gave a very important award to Warren Winiarski, the founder of Stag's Leap, a wonderful man and good friend of papá's. My father was always grateful for what Warren did for New World wine.

AV: How could one not remember Warren Winiarski! The last time I saw him was during the wildfires. It was terrifying, because the fire reached the gates of the vineyard, and it was a miracle that the vines were spared.

LC: My father loved to tell this story about his grandfather Nicola. Nicola was a fanatic of Argentina and believed that great wines could be made here. But he always cautioned his grandson, my father, against trying to compete with the French. Because they had something special called *terroir*, something that nobody else had. I think that at the Judgment of Paris, California demonstrated that *terroir*, or the taste of place, could also exist outside of France, and specifically in the New World. I think this was the most important outcome of the tasting: that *terroir* was not the property of France.

AV: And later we had our own Judgment of Paris...

LC: Yes, a tasting we entered into with great fear in our hearts. It was Nicolás Catena Zapata 1997 up against Solaia, Château Latour, Haut-Brion, Caymus Special Selection and Opus One, all from the 1997 vintage. Miraculously and to our great surprise, Nicolás Catena Zapata came out at the top in all the tastings except for the one where it came in second.

AV: This new confidence helped us in our dream and mission to find new soils and regions for our vineyards in Argentina. There was a newfound feeling that we could compete, and that we had just as good a *terroir* as any other fine-wine-producing country. What we really need now is to continue to acquire expertise every time we plant in a new place; we must continue to do research, lots and lots of research.

LC: We also discovered that not just any region or vineyard in Mendoza can compete with the *Grands Crus*. We have to seek out and identify those "one of a kind" vineyards, like Adrianna, and not even all of Adrianna.

AV: Yes, and it's usually only a small proportion of a vineyard that can compete with the best. It's the same in France.

LC: Yes, that was Argentina's mistake before.... People said: "Oh this whole area, this whole vineyard..." when throughout the history of wine it's been small parcels in just the right spot that produce a *Grand Cru* quality wine.

AV: Five years ago I was invited to a tasting with very important wine people from Mendoza, and when I started talking about *parcelas* (vineyard parcels), a lot of them actually got angry.

LC: Because they thought you were being elitist...

AV: Exactly! But I wasn't, quite the opposite in fact.

LC: Yes, it's quite the opposite. Some things are just better than others.

AV: Yes, or different.

LC: Right, it's not like there aren't excellent table wines, for instance. There are plenty of delicious wines that aren't expensive. But for a wine to be suitable for aging fifty or sixty years, it has to be produced in a "one of a kind" place that delivers a "one of a kind" flavor.

AV: Right, the gold in the vineyards.

LC: Oh yes, "Gold in the Vineyards" like the name of my book! Speaking of which, it was Steven Spurrier, the journalist who organized the 1976 Judgment of Paris who wrote the text for the back cover. It all comes together, doesn't it? What were we doing in '76?

AV: At that time in Argentina we had about 50,000 or 56,000 hectares of Malbec, which was usually blended with lighter criolla grapes.

LC: Of course, at that time Argentina didn't want to compete with the rest of the world; we wanted to drink all our wine here, at home.

AV: We were once the biggest importers of wines from Bordeaux.

LC: That's right! In the early 20th century the biggest importer of wines from Bordeaux was Argentina, because quality wine has always been central to the Argentine table.

Dear Alejandro, Please find enclosed this lovely Polaroid we took from the Adrianna lookout in the middle of the night, which made me think of something you like to say: "Everything comes down to our interior journey; it's this journey inwards that is reflected in our wines." Hugs, Laura

Exports of this new style of Argentine wines met with great success in the USA and in the UK. Argentina had begun to make wines that met international standards.

Some years later, Nicolás Catena had another revelation, this time while having dinner with well-known French oenologist and consultant Jacques Lurton in Bordeaux. Upon tasting a wine from a traditional area of Mendoza, Jacques commented that the wine had no flaws, but that it made him think of a wine from the Languedoc. A warm area in the south of France, the Languedoc is generally not held in very high regard by the Bordeaux producers. The comment could be even perceived as an insult, especially coming from a Bordeaux producer. And Catena, who aspired to make wines at the level of the best Bordeaux reds, concluded that he would need to go to cooler climates (as cool as Bordeaux) in order to farm grapes that would yield the highest quality wines. In other words, he needed to abide by the French dictum that correlates a wine's quality to its terroir. No machine or advanced technology would make his wine dream possible, unless the grapes were sourced from an ideal *terroir* with the optimal soil and climate. This is what led Nicolás Catena to plant vineyards in the coolest parts of Mendoza and to explore higher-altitude regions in the foothills of the Andes Mountains.

IN 1992, CATENA PURCHASED A PLOT OF LAND IN GUALTALLARY, TUPUNGATO ALTO, THAT WOULD COME TO BE KNOWN AS THE ADRIANNA VINEYARD. BECAUSE OF ITS HIGH-ALTITUDE LOCATION AT ALMOST 5,000 FEET ELEVATION, AND EXTREME COOL CLIMATE, THE SITE WAS NOT CONSIDERED SUITABLE FOR VITICULTURE AT THE TIME. OVER THE YEARS, HOWEVER, THE ADRIANNA VINEYARD WOULD COME TO BE KNOWN AS SOUTH AMERICA'S "GRAND CRU" VINEYARD BECAUSE OF ITS HIGHLY RATED WINES.

The Adrianna Vineyard weather station registers its climate as falling in Zones I and II on the Winkler scale, making it the equivalent of Burgundy or a very cold part of Bordeaux. Despite warnings from his head of viticulture that only sparkling grapes would ripen in this location, and never a red variety such as Malbec, Catena decided to plant Malbec here. Catena was obsessed with exploring the cool-climate limit of vine cultivation in Mendoza, and he was counting on the increased sunlight at high altitude. He hypothesized that the intense mountain sun would allow for the maturation of a relatively late-ripening variety such as Malbec. In 1996, when the first harvest from Adrianna was vinified and the wines were tasted, they caused quite a stir, especially the Malbec. The wine was dense and complex, yet extremely velvety, with a low pH, high natural acidity and intense violet aromatics.

During the early stages of high-altitude microclimate exploration, Catena hired the Italian oenologist Attilio Pagli to help locate an ideal location to grow Sangiovese in Mendoza. When Pagli encountered the Catena family's old Malbec vineyards in La Consulta and Lunlunta, however, it was love at first sight. Pagli advised Catena to focus on Malbec and joined the Catena team in 1992. The Malbec they made in 1994, intensely aromatic, concentrated and smooth, impressed everybody so much that Nicolás decided to bottle it under the name Angélica Zapata, in honor of his mother. The success obtained with the old-vine Malbec from Lunlunta and, later on, the fresh, elegant Malbecs of the high-altitude Adrianna vineyard convinced Nicolás once and for all that the grape had great potential.

In the 1990s, Argentine wineries started hiring prestigious wine consultants with the goal of elevating wine quality and improving their competitiveness in the export markets. The famous French winemaker Michel Rolland acted as consultant for Pernod Ricard, Etchart and Clos de los Siete, where he also became a partner. Renowned Italian oenologist Alberto Antonini, co-owner of Altos las Hormigas, advised several other wineries, including Bodega Melipal, Zuccardi and Bodega Chacana.

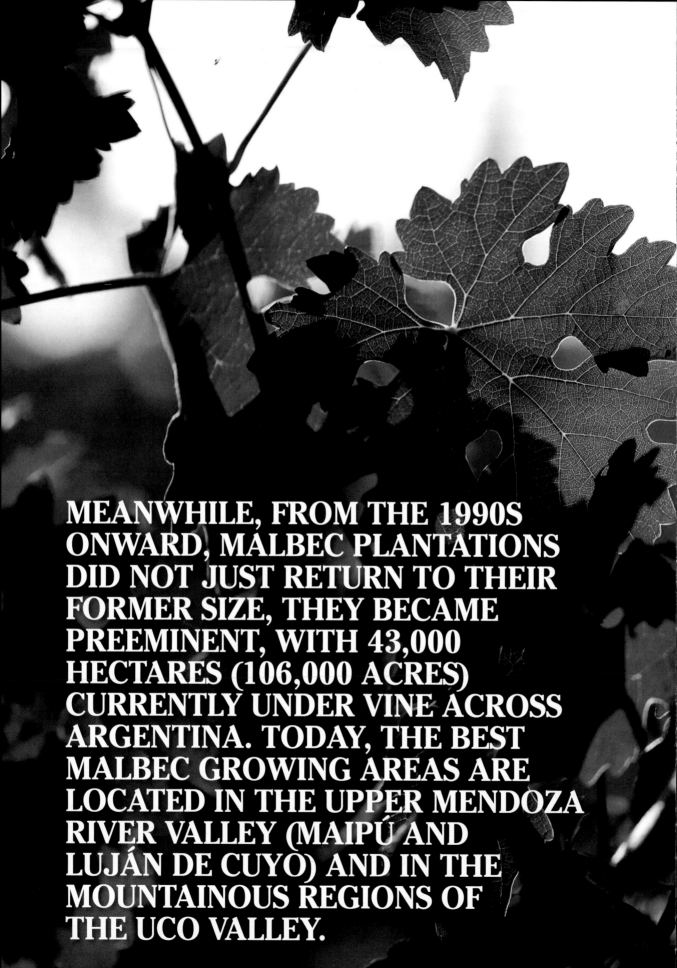

MEANWHILE, FROM THE 1990S ONWARD, MALBEC PLANTATIONS DID NOT JUST RETURN TO THEIR FORMER SIZE, THEY BECAME PREEMINENT, WITH 43,000 HECTARES (106,000 ACRES) CURRENTLY UNDER VINE ACROSS ARGENTINA. TODAY, THE BEST MALBEC GROWING AREAS ARE LOCATED IN THE UPPER MENDOZA RIVER VALLEY (MAIPÚ AND LUJÁN DE CUYO) AND IN THE MOUNTAINOUS REGIONS OF THE UCO VALLEY.

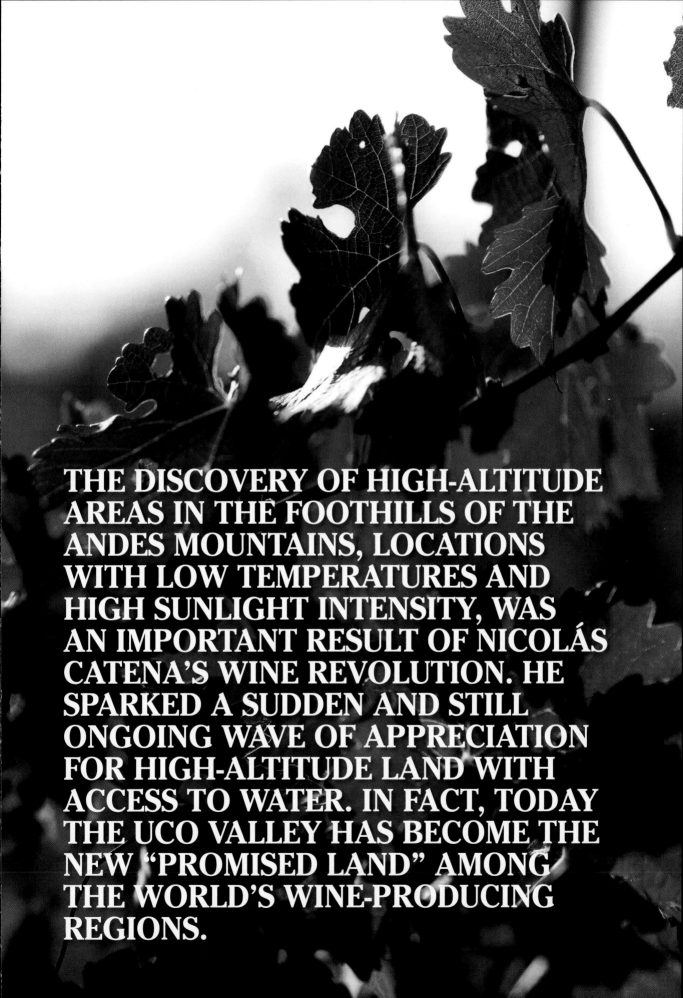

THE DISCOVERY OF HIGH-ALTITUDE AREAS IN THE FOOTHILLS OF THE ANDES MOUNTAINS, LOCATIONS WITH LOW TEMPERATURES AND HIGH SUNLIGHT INTENSITY, WAS AN IMPORTANT RESULT OF NICOLÁS CATENA'S WINE REVOLUTION. HE SPARKED A SUDDEN AND STILL ONGOING WAVE OF APPRECIATION FOR HIGH-ALTITUDE LAND WITH ACCESS TO WATER. IN FACT, TODAY THE UCO VALLEY HAS BECOME THE NEW "PROMISED LAND" AMONG THE WORLD'S WINE-PRODUCING REGIONS.

Published works by the Catena Institute of Wine in collaboration with local researchers have shown that high-altitude conditions create a unique microclimate for Mendoza's vineyards: lower average daily and nightly temperatures, and an increase in sunlight intensity.

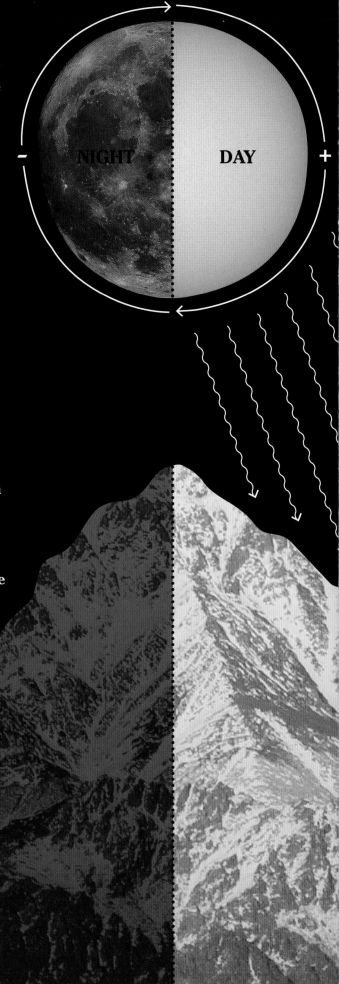

1) Lower average temperatures

Thanks to lower mean temperatures, vines planted at higher altitudes are protected from heat stress. The grapes are allowed to slowly accumulate sugars and polyphenols, and to retain an optimal amount of malic acid, so important for wine texture. This all translates into wines with great concentration, heightened acidity and overall freshness and balance. Additionally, the lower vineyard temperatures drastically slow down the ripening process, meaning that between veraison (when the grapes change color) and ripening, high-altitude vines accumulate more polyphenols (tannins, flavors and color). The cool microclimates found at altitude slow down the final stage of the ripening process, when the sugar accumulates. This combination of factors results in elegant wines with excellent concentration of flavors, optimal acidity and moderate (not too high) alcohol levels.

2) Lower night-time temperatures

In cooler high-altitude areas where daily temperatures don't usually rise above 30°C (86°F), photosynthetic activity is more constant than in warmer areas. By the same token, the much lower temperatures (generally lower than 12°C or 54°F) at night allow the plant to "come to a stop" and "rest" with no extra effort, so the composite of flavors and aromas produced during the day can come together. This gradual ripening between day and night results in higher-quality grapes with optimal acidity and enhanced aromatics.

3) More intense sunlight

The levels of sunlight intensity found in Mendoza's mountain vineyards are among the highest of any viticultural region in the world. The vine perceives the enhanced ultraviolet rays as a threat or stress factor. And therefore, to protect her "children," the seeds, the vine increases the production of antioxidant compounds in its skins, like a mother applying sunscreen to her baby. Given that most of the polyphenols are contained in the grape skins, we can conclude that the very intense sunlight leads to berries with a higher concentration of tannins and color compounds. This all translates into intense wines with great aging potential. Among antioxidant components present in grape skins that increase with sunlight, resveratrol has been studied by medical researchers for its potential health benefits.

THE INTENSITY OF MOUNTAIN SUNLIGHT PROVOKES A RESPONSE IN THE PLANT: THE VINE PROTECTS ITS SEEDS BY INCREASING THE ANTIOXIDANT POLYPHENOLS IN ITS SKINS— THE PLANT EQUIVALENT OF SUNSCREEN.

The Winkler Scale and the micro-climates of Mendoza

The Winkler Index is used to describe regional climates for viticulture. For each day from October 1 to April 30 (in the Southern Hemisphere), calculate the number of degrees by which the average temperature is above 10 degrees Celsius (high temperature + low temperature divided by 2 then subtract 10 degrees). Then add each day to get the total degree-days for each growing season.

REGION	CLASSIFICATION	NUMBER OF DEGREE-DAYS IN °C
I	Cool	<1389 °C
II	Cool-Temperate	>1389<1667 °C
III	Warm-Temperate	>1667<1944 °C
IV	Warm	>1944<2222 °C
V	Hot	>2222 °C

LOCAL AREAS	INTERNATIONAL REGIONS
Higher parts of Gualtallary **> 5,000 f.a.s.l.**	**Burgundy, Champagne**
Gualtallary **4,250 f.a.s.l. up to 5,000 f.a.s.l.**	**Bordeaux, Barolo, Côte-Rôtie**
El Cepillo, Paraje Altamira, **Agrelo, Villa Bastías** **3,600 f.a.s.l. To 4,250 f.a.s.l.**	**Napa Valley, Chianti Classico,** **Côtes du Rhône, Rioja**
Lunlunta **2,500 f.a.s.l. to 3,050 f.a.s.l.**	**Châteauneuf-du-Pape**
Eastern Mendoza **(Rivadavia, San Martín, Junín)** **2,000 to 2,500 f.a.s.l.**	**Jerez-Xéres-Sherry**

La Pirámide Vineyard, Agrelo

CATENA'S
MASSAL AND CLONAL SELECTIONS

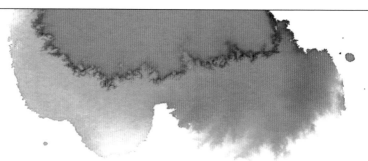

In addition to discovering new, higher areas in the foothills of the Andes Mountains, in the early 1990s Nicolás Catena Zapata also decided to implement a rigorous study and selection of Malbec plants, known today as the Catena Cuttings.

Catena had been able to import to Argentina the best selections of Cabernet Sauvignon and Chardonnay plants available in France and in the USA. But when it came to Malbec, he realized that nobody in Argentina or elsewhere had undertaken a serious plant selection. He was convinced that a rigorous study of Mendoza Malbec was needed as part of the effort to elevate the quality of Argentine Malbec on Argentine soil.

Historically, Argentine Malbec vineyards had been planted with informally sourced cuttings. A producer planting a new vineyard would take cuttings from his own or a neighbor's vineyard, making a rough selection simply by visually inspecting each vine. Vineyards planted in this manner were typically very heterogeneous and uneven in terms of ripening time and vine characteristics. The Malbec selection carried out by the Catena Institute under Dr. Laura Catena's leadership consisted of isolating and then multiplying individual plants with certain valuable characteristics from within the Malbec population (well-balanced plants with low yields, smaller bunches and berries were considered best for quality and concentration).

The process of planting a vineyard requires significant patience and planning, from the selection and multiplication of

From: Catena, Laura

To: Vigil, Alejandro

Subject: The team at the Catena Institute

Hi Alejandro,

It's amazing that we were published in the *American Journal of Enology and Viticulture*! Fernando Buscema's experience at the University of California at Davis shows how important it is not to lock ourselves away in our own little world, to actually open up to what's going on outside of Argentina. There were clear differences between the Malbec from California and the Malbec from Mendoza—what are your thoughts? Why do you think the California Malbec was more herbaceous? Is it perhaps because they have planted the Côt variety of Malbec, and not our pre-phylloxeric selections? Maybe it's the Mendoza sun, or something about our soils and climate that reduces herbal qualities. Or maybe it's a mix of factors. Let me know when you can talk on WhatsApp. If possible, call me tomorrow at noon your time.

Hugs,
Laura

cuttings to the layout of posts and trellis wires to the three-year wait for the first usable harvest. It requires a long-term vision, a commitment to soil, climate and plant research and a desire to make singularly unforgettable wines. Catena's Malbec massal and clonal selection, the Catena Cuttings, was the founding project of the Catena Institute of Wine in 1995. It gave birth to the Institute's vision of "using science to preserve the nature and the viticultural traditions of Argentina."

The three stages of the Catena plant selection process:

1. In 1995 Laura Catena founded the Catena Institute of Wine and began selecting 135 plants with different qualities from an old Catena family vineyard (planted ninety years ago in Lunlunta, Maipú) and other vineyards in the Province of Mendoza managed by the Universidad Nacional de Cuyo and INTA (Argentine Institute of Agricultural Technology). These 135 plants were reproduced from cuttings and then planted, four selections per row, in the La Pirámide vineyard, which surrounds the Catena Zapata winery in Agrelo, Luján de Cuyo. This first selection of Malbec plants, called "massal," has been replicated in the Catena vineyards and replanted in the family's newer plots to ensure the survival of the original population. The selection was planted in Catena's Adrianna vineyard in Gualtallary at almost 5,000-feet elevation to study the effect of altitude on the plants' behavior.

2. During the second phase, in 1996, a selection was made of the fifteen best plants from among the original 135. Those

chosen had low yields, small clusters, high concentration of polyphenols and low likelihood of millerandage. They also had different but complementary flavor profiles. Microvinifications of each individual plant selection were made in order to properly evaluate and compare their characteristics: aromas, concentration, natural acidity, ripening point, level of astringency and sensory profile.

3. In 1997 five plants were chosen from among the fifteen selected the previous year and sent to the University of Adelaide in Australia where they were certified as being free of vineyard viruses.

Today, Catena Zapata has the largest selection of Malbec plants in the world. The Catena Institute evaluates their behavior with every vintage.

"THE CATENA INSTITUTE WAS WHERE I STARTED OUT AT CATENA. IN FACT, I GOT THE JOB BECAUSE THEY WERE LOOKING FOR A SOIL SPECIALIST AND I WAS THEN IN CHARGE OF THE SOIL RESEARCH DEPARTMENT AT INTA (ARGENTINE INSTITUTE OF AGRICULTURAL TECHNOLOGY). SOIL HAS ALWAYS BEEN MY AREA OF INTEREST. TODAY, AT THE CATENA INSTITUTE, WE ARE WORKING ON MANY DIFFERENT FIELDS OF RESEARCH, FROM STUDYING HOW MALBEC AGES TO THE COMPLEX QUESTION OF HOW SOIL AND CLIMATE INTERACT IN DIFFERENT REGIONS AND PARCELAS [VINEYARD PARCELS]. THE WORK WE ARE DOING IS, IN MY OPINION, AMONG THE MOST RELEVANT IN THE WORLD OF WINE TODAY."

ALEJANDRO VIGIL

THE HISTORY OF
THE CATENA INSTITUTE

1853
The first Malbec vines are planted in Argentina.

1984
Nicolás Catena's wine revolution begins: he sets the goal of making Argentine wines that can stand with the best of the world.

1995
Under the leadership of Dr. Laura Catena, a selection of 135 Malbec plants from the Angélica Vineyard, known as the Catena Cuttings, becomes the founding project of the Catena Institute of Wine.

1932
The second generation, led by Domingo Vicente Catena, master of the blend, discovers the Uco Valley as the best source of Malbec in Mendoza.

1902
Italian vintner Nicola Catena plants his first Malbec vines in Mendoza. The Catena Zapata wine tradition is born.

1992
Nicolás Catena dares to plant a vineyard in Gualtallary some 5,000 feet above sea level, an altitude where vines had never been planted before.

1968
Nicolás Catena Zapata and his father Domingo's Saint Felicien Cabernet Sauvignon becomes Argentina's most collectable red wine.

1995 onwards
Meteorological stations are placed in all the Catena vineyards, at different altitudes, to study the effects of altitude on climate

2007
Director of the Catena Institute Fernando Buscema establishes partnerships between the Catena Institute and local research institutions such as the National University of Cuyo to study Malbec cultivation and sustainability.

2002-2004
Soil specialist Alejandro Vigil and Dr. Laura Catena begin the work of *parcela* (vineyard parcel) selection at the Catena Institute. Together with the School of Agriculture in Mendoza, research begins into the effect of altitude and sunlight intensity on Mendoza's high mountain vineyards.

2014
Research carried out by the Catena Institute and U.C. Davis (Buscema and Boulton) produces the most extensive study of Malbec ever undertaken. The results are published in *Food Chemistry* and the *American Journal of Enology and Viticulture*.

2012
The Catena Institute develops the first Argentine wine sustainability protocol in partnership with Bodegas de Argentina.

2008
Catena Zapata's *parcela* revolution: following an in-depth study of all the parcelas of the Adrianna Vineyard, the first Chardonnay vintage from a parcela is made and bottled.

2021
The Catena Institute and CONICET (Argentina's National Research Council) co-publish in "Scientific Reports" (a Nature publication) the most extensive *terroir* chemistry study ever undertaken. Lead researcher Roy Urvieta studied 23 Malbec vineyards and showed *terroir* differences over three years, down to the individual parcela.

2005 onwards
The Catena family begins to study and plant vineyards in regions outside of Mendoza: Salta, La Rioja and Patagonia.

2013 onwards
Research studies are undertaken to study soil micro-biome, parcela soil composition and its effect on wine flavors and aromas, Malbec ageability, phylloxera, new grape varietals and Bonarda plant selections. Research collaborations are established with U.C. Davis and the University of Burgundy.

6

The Importance of *Terroir*

THE GEOLOGY
OF MENDOZA

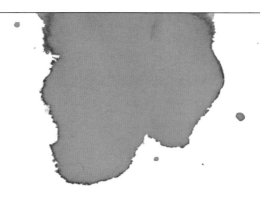

Origins

The high-altitude vineyards of Mendoza, in the foothills of the Andes Mountains, are unique because of their elevation, southern latitude, slope and mixed alluvial and colluvial origins. "Alluvial" describes soil material that was—and continues to be—transported by water, while "colluvial" means material driven down the mountain by the forces of gravity. These geological origins make our soils especially suitable for viticulture of the highest level.

The Andes Mountains have ancient origins. As the largest active mountain range in the world, the Andes run as far north as Venezuela and down through Colombia, Ecuador, Peru, Bolivia, Chile and Argentina, where they form the western border of Mendoza Province. The Andes contain several of the highest mountains on the planet, including Aconcagua, whose peak is 22,800 feet above sea level

(f.a.s.l.) and sectors with active volcanoes. The areas containing vineyards range from 1,600 f.a.s.l. to 5,400 f.a.s.l.

The Andes mountain range formed from the global movements of tectonic plates and a potent mix of geologic processes occurring over millions of years and still in motion today. The separation of the supercontinent Pangea and its lower part, Gondwana, began the formation and positioning of the present continents. About 485 million years ago, in the Early Paleozoic Era, the central-west region of Argentina became a proto-margin, or rudimentary margin—the foundation, in other words, for a future mountain range.

In the Late Paleozoic period, Gondwanides, the first mountain range along the Pacific border, was formed by a subduction event. Subsequently, in the Mesozoic Era, between 150 and

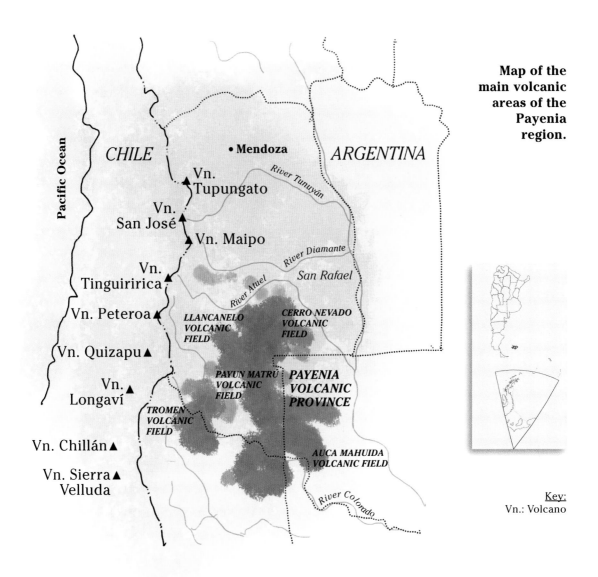

Pacific Ocean

CHILE • Mendoza ARGENTINA

River Tunuyán

Vn. Tupungato

Vn. San José

Vn. Maipo

River Diamante

San Rafael

Vn. Tinguiririca

River Atuel

Vn. Peteroa

LLANCANELO VOLCANIC FIELD

CERRO NEVADO VOLCANIC FIELD

Vn. Quizapu

Vn. Longaví

PAYUN MATRÚ VOLCANIC FIELD

PAYENIA VOLCANIC PROVINCE

TROMEN VOLCANIC FIELD

Vn. Chillán

AUCA MAHUIDA VOLCANIC FIELD

Vn. Sierra Velluda

River Colorado

Key:
Vn.: Volcano

115 million years ago, the pre-Andean elevations expanded from north to south. This process culminated in the collision of the Oceanic Nazca plate with the South American plate about 20 million years ago, which caused significant tectonic and volcanic activity and lifted up the Andes. The present-day Andes was fully established by the beginning of the Pliocene Age, about 5 million years ago. Today the Andes Mountain range contains sections that once lay under the sea and others that were former volcanoes. Where most of the vineyards of Mendoza are located are sedimentary areas arising from the transport of materials down from the mountain.

THE VOLCANIC ROCKS THAT MAKE UP THE ANDES ARE OLDER THAN THE ANDES MOUNTAIN RANGE ITSELF.

About 150–115 million years ago

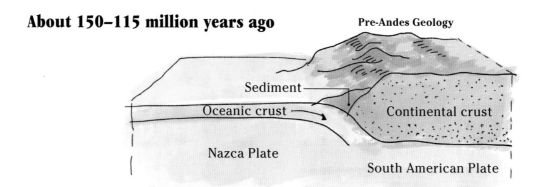

Pre-Andes Geology

Sediment
Oceanic crust
Continental crust
Nazca Plate
South American Plate

20 Million Years Ago

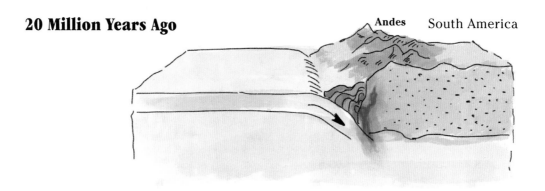

Andes   South America

Image representing the collision between the Nazca oceanic plate and the South American plate, which gave rise to the Andes Mountain Range

Since then, violent earthquakes, volcanic eruptions, the melting of glaciers into rivers and streams, erosion and eolic activity have contributed to the development of a wide-ranging variety of soils and climates, from very warm (in the lowest areas) to very cold (in the highest), all within relatively small distances. In a span of just 40 miles of Mendoza foothills (from Lulunta to Tupungato), the climate varies significantly, as much as it would in regions close to sea level over hundreds of miles. For example, the temperature differential between Mendoza's Lunlunta (warmer) and Tupungato (colder) is as great as that between the southern Rhône and Champagne, two French wine regions that lie 300 miles apart.

The origin of Mendoza's soils

Most of Mendoza's soils are alluvial in origin. Sediments originating in the mountains were transported by rivers and melting glaciers and spread out in alluvial fans. In some sectors of the Mendoza foothills, these alluvial fans are superimposed or interlocked; others are spread as wide as 3,000 feet. The farther east you travel from the Andes, the more eolic the soil formations; "eolic" meaning that it originated from materials deposited by the wind. You'll also find colluvial soils at the edges of some alluvial cones, as in the southwestern part of El Cepillo.

The mineral composition of materials transported by mountain rivers reflects the geologic diversity of the regions they traverse. In the same alluvial cone,

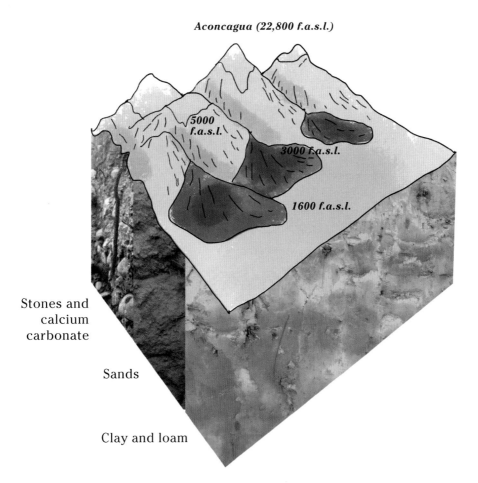

Aconcagua (22,800 f.a.s.l.)

5000 f.a.s.l.

3000 f.a.s.l.

1600 f.a.s.l.

Stones and calcium carbonate

Sands

Clay and loam

Simplified image of alluvial fan: soils and textures at different altitudes.

for example, you might find rocks of volcanic (basalt), plutonic (granite) and sedimentary (calcareous) origin.

How does an alluvial fan form? The development of an alluvial fan doesn't happen overnight. This complex process involves the accumulation of a diverse range of materials over a long period of time. Loose rocks driven down a mountain by gravity or avalanches break up and crumble as they move along. Smaller materials such as sand and clay are carried down by water.

Once an alluvial cone is formed, new waterways may generate channels within an existing alluvial fan and form additional layers of sedimentary deposit.

Hundreds of feet deep lie underground aquifers with significant water reserves that are regularly replenished by the melting of Andean glaciers and snow.

Soil texture

Soils formed by alluvial fans tend to be less fertile higher up, closer to their point of origin. This is where soils contain greater quantities of rocks and stones and are generally poor, with lower water retention. As we move farther away from the mountain and the cone grows larger, the water loses energy and the composition of the soil becomes finer, made up of materials such as sand, silt and, finally, clay. Here the cone also becomes deeper, more fertile and retains more water.

The soils in the plains tend to be deep and fertile and are preferred for growing fruits and vegetables. The grapevine, on the

MENDOZA'S CLASSIC ALLUVIAL FORMATION BEGAN WITH A GLACIER.

Materials as large as enormous blocks of stone were dragged down by glaciers, and the surfaces of the stones were eroded by glacial meltwaters until they became angular or rounded.

At its origin, water traveled down from the glacier through a single canal. When the canal was blocked by the stones it was carrying, water would infiltrate to contiguous areas. Then, as the quantity of water became reduced, the strength of the current would diminish and leave larger stones in the higher altitudes. Pebbles and smaller stones would settle in the middle heights, and sands would drift down to the base of the cones. In the lowest areas clays would sediment in a lake formation.

other hand, is a climber used to struggling, and adapts well to low-fertility, well-drained, gravely soils as well as to the somewhat more fertile loessic (silt and clay) soils in the plains. Each type of soil gives rise to wines with different characteristics. Vineyard soils are generally formed by a mixture of sand, silt and clay, known as loam. Depending on the dominant material, the soil is referred to as clay-loam, silt-loam or sandy-loam. The gravel content is generally greater and the stones larger at the higher altitudes. It is, however, impossible to generalize about soil texture: eolic (wind) deposits, seismic activity (giving rise to hill formation over time), volcanic eruptions and even the drying up or change in the course of a river or stream can significantly alter a given site's soil texture at any altitude. Soils with a high gravel-and-stone content such as those in the upper parts of the Uco Valley tend to have better drainage; vines are less vigorous and yields are naturally low; botrytis and rot are almost nonexistent. Surface stones heat up during the day and cool off significantly at night, thus creating a very specific microclimate for each grape cluster. Low yields and cold mountain nights give rise to concentrated grapes that ripen slowly and reach harvest time with optimal levels of natural acidity. Some of the most famous wines in the world come from areas with gravelly soils, such as parts of the Rhône, Pomerol and Pauillac. Additionally, the gravelly soils of the Uco Valley have high levels of calcium carbonate or limestone, particularly those of Gualtallary and Tupungato Alto in western Uco, and those of Paraje Altamira, La Consulta and El Cepillo in southern Uco.

**Soil texture
classification triangle**

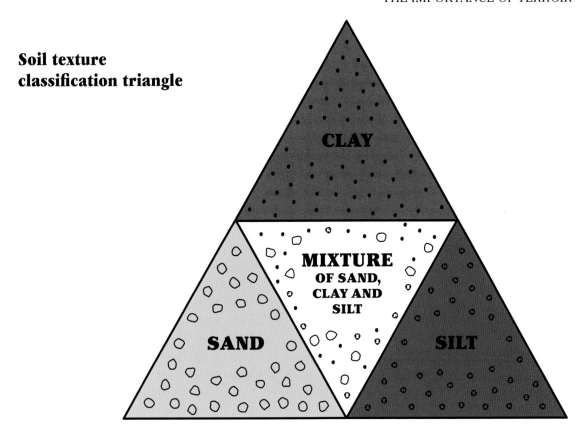

Size of the particles

CLAY	SILT	SAND
0,0002 mm	0,0002 - 0,05 mm	0,05 - 2 mm

Soil scientists believe that thin layers of water form within calcium carbonate-rich soils, encouraging protective microflora that help shelter the vines from the stress of drought and heat. These "happier vines" growing in calcium carbonate-rich soils are thus able to produce useful acids and aromas that impart minerality to the wines. Some of the world's most classically elegant wines are produced in areas rich in limestone or calcium carbonate, such as Burgundy, Châteauneuf du Pape, Gigondas, Barolo, Montalcino and Ribera del Duero. Clay-rich soils, on the other hand, which are prevalent in Luján de Cuyo and in lower-altitude areas, tend to retain significantly more water than sandy or stony soils and are at greater risk of suffering from rot in wet years. But there are benefits to having clay soils in a region as dry as Mendoza:

the greater water retention can have a cooling effect on the vines, imparting texture and density on the mid-palate. The presence of clay is prized in many famous wine regions such as Ribera del Duero in Spain, Saint-Émilion in Bordeaux and Vosne-Romanée in Burgundy.

How we study soil

First, a vineyard soil survey is done to identify homogeneous areas. This can be done with electro-conductive technology or by taking soil-depth samples. After identifying consistent areas, soil-pits are dug up in each *parcela* (vineyard parcel). These pits tend to be of shallow to medium depth (up to 2m by 1m on the surface and 2m in depth), which allows us to study the different soil layers. Each soil layer is described visually, and its chemical

Soil profile on the banks of the Mendoza River. Angélica Vineyard, property of the Catena Zapata family, planted between 1920 and 1930.

makeup is studied to determine texture and water retention. The volume, depth and thickness of roots is also measured.

Electrical conductivity analysis

Electrical conductivity measurements help us map out vineyard soils and identify homogeneous areas. The result of these measurements is a map of polygons representing areas of high and low conductivity. This information alone doesn't tell us much, because a number of different factors can affect the data: some sectors of the soil might be more saline, some might have more clay, some might be wetter, and some might contain fewer stones, all of which can result in higher electrical conductivity. This is why after creating an electrical conductivity map,

we go straight to the vineyard to explore *why* there are differences among the vines, even in areas with similar electrical conductivity. In general, higher values of electrical conductivity mean greater water retention or deeper soils, but in order to understand what this means for the vine's roots, we need to dig soil pits.

What we know about our roots

In Mendoza, roots have been found at a depth greater than nine feet in both deep and stony soils. Main roots (greater than 5 mm in diameter) are located in the first layer of soil down to 10-45cm. These thicker roots have difficulty getting through hard limestone layers or between rocks that are joined together by calcium carbonate. Fine roots (less than 1 mm in width) have

**Detail of thick and fine roots
in rocky soils, Uco Valley**

the greatest water and nutrient absorption capacity; they spread deeply and widely across soil layers (horizons). Rocky soils have greater numbers of these fine roots, an indication that the vines may be fighting harder to survive the extreme conditions.

Minerals in the soil

No clear-cut relationship has been established between soil mineral composition and wine characteristics. Minerals in the soil affect the vine depending on their availability—trouble arises when a soil has too much or too little of a given mineral. Nitrogen and potassium are the most relevant: the former is a nutrient that influences plant vigor, the latter can affect must and wine pH (acidity). Soils with high salinity,

greater than 1.5 dS/m, may provoke stress on the vine. Water can be applied to vines growing in saline soils as a way to mitigate sodium toxicity. In certain places, however, high salinity may be an essential part of the local flavor. Researchers in Sicily, for example, have found that for the Nero d'Avola grape, salinity values of between 1 and 7.6 dS/m in the soil are typical of the most appreciated wines, possibly imparting more intense color, fruity aromas and saline flavor. Meanwhile, Nero d'Avola wines coming from soils with lower salinity (0.7dS/m) have been described as flat and insipid. The bottom line: we still don't know how to explain the relationship between a wine's mineral aromas and the mineral contents of the soil where it is grown. What we do know, however, is that experienced

Left: a spider in Gualtallary.

Right: Diagram showing soil and surface microorganisms.

winemakers and viticulturists recognize very specific flavors and textures in wines made from different soils, which leads many a winemaker to believe that a certain mineral character in wine can be traced to the minerals in the soil. In summary, we still don't know how to explain the relationship between the mineral aromas found in a wine and the minerals in the soil from which it grew.

The microbiome in the soil and in the wine

The vineyard microbiome has only recently began to receive attention from wine researchers. Studies carried out by the Catena Institute in collaboration with the EU's Microwine show that the vineyard microbiome can vary significantly not only at different altitudes, but also among adjacent parcels in one vineyard.

The microbiome includes mycorrhiza (fungi), rhizobacteria (which help the vine tolerate stress and absorb nutrients and minerals) and yeasts (which have an effect on native yeast fermentations). It is likely that the vineyard microbiome has a far greater effect on the flavor of a wine (or *goût de terroir*) than previously thought. And the soil microbiome is likely to be particularly relevant in poor soils—with low organic-matter content—such as those of the Uco Valley in Mendoza. Until recently it had been difficult to study the soil microbiome since less than 10% of the soil's microorganisms could be cultured in the lab. Today, thanks to DNA sequencing techniques—similar to those used to rapidly sequence human DNA—we are beginning to understand in much greater detail the presence and effect of microbes on soils and their crops.

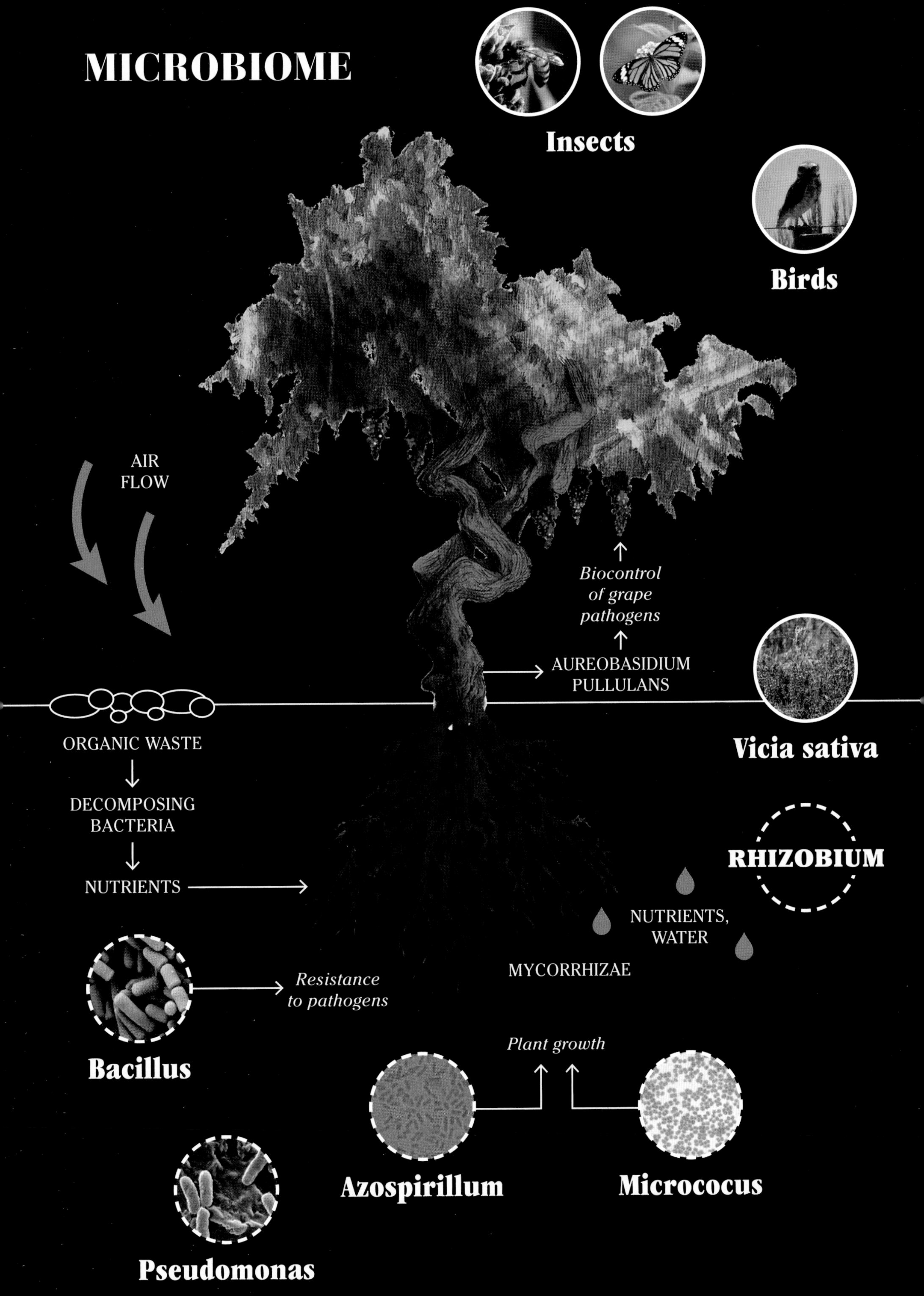

MICROBIOME

Insects

Birds

AIR
FLOW

*Biocontrol
of grape
pathogens*

AUREOBASIDIUM
PULLULANS

Vicia sativa

ORGANIC WASTE

↓

DECOMPOSING
BACTERIA

↓

NUTRIENTS ⟶

RHIZOBIUM

NUTRIENTS,
WATER

MYCORRHIZAE

*Resistance
to pathogens*

Bacillus

Plant growth

Azospirillum

Micrococus

Pseudomonas

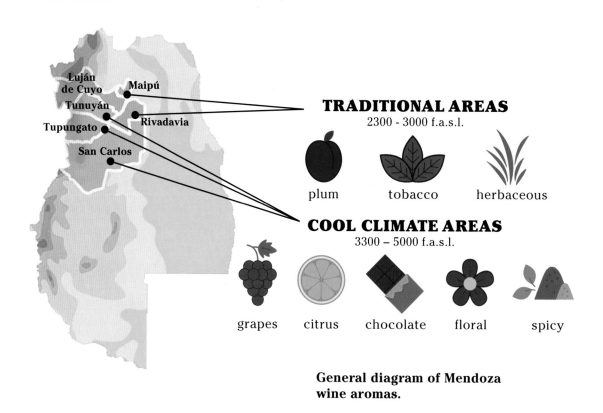

TRADITIONAL AREAS
2300 - 3000 f.a.s.l.

plum   tobacco   herbaceous

COOL CLIMATE AREAS
3300 – 5000 f.a.s.l.

grapes   citrus   chocolate   floral   spicy

General diagram of Mendoza
wine aromas.

AGRICULTURE IN MENDOZA EXISTS THANKS TO FIVE RIVERS FORMED BY THE MELTING ANDEAN GLACIERS: THE RIVERS MENDOZA, TUNUYÁN, DIAMANTE, ATUEL AND MALARGÜE.

The big question we vintners ask ourselves

Since the Middle Ages, when Cistercian monks in Burgundy identified the *goût de terroir*, or taste of place, we have known that the flavor of a wine varies according to the soil where the vines are grown and to the climate of each vintage. It is difficult to correlate the particular chemical composition of a wine with its flavor, however. And we are only just beginning to understand the chemical explanation for flavor differences among wines: differences between vineyards and regions, and differences between one vintage and the next. Ultimately, what matters is what wine drinkers perceive—and that is why "sensory analysis," a methodology based on the human nose and palate, can be used along with chemical analysis to understand the differences between wines from different terroirs.

Regional breakdown of the aromas of Mendoza wines

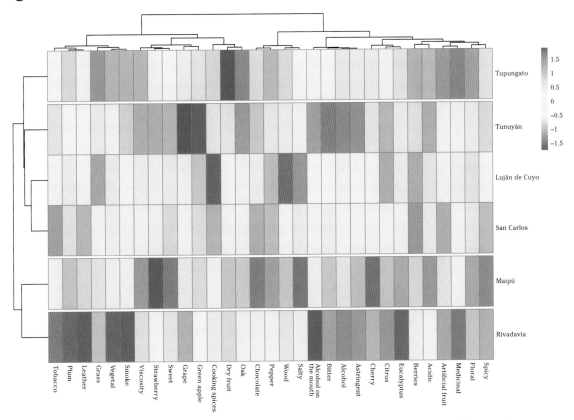

Heat map representing the aromatic descriptors of Maipú, Tupungato, Tunuyán, Luján de Cuyo, San Carlos and Rivadavia. Source: Catena Institute and Heymann Lab, UC Davis. Unpublished data.

Sensory evaluation of wine, the heat map

At the Catena Institute we have created a "sensory panel" made up of teams of people with sensory aroma training. Our findings indicate that wines have a distinctive sensory fingerprint unique to the various regions, and also specific to different soils in neighboring parcels.

These sensory wine descriptors are illustrated in a heat map. The map represents the statistic analysis of sensory data highlighting the dominant descriptors of each wine and region. The scale goes from red to blue: red "heat" refers to a particular descriptor found at high levels, and blue represents "less heat," referring to descriptors found at lower levels.

WILL WE EVER BE ABLE TO DISCERN THE REAL EFFECT OF THE SOIL ON THE FLAVOR OF OUR WINES, WHICH DIFFER GREATLY DEPENDING ON THE CHARACTERISTICS OF EACH REGION, VINEYARD AND PARCEL?

Adrianna Vineyard, Gualtallary, Uco Valley. Vines protected by hail netting.

For example, the wines of Maipú present greater levels of viscosity, strawberry, sweet, cherry and oak aromas (reds on the heat map) and lower levels of saline, astringent, floral, bitter and spicy sensory components (blues/light blues on the heat map).

The surface area planted with Malbec in Mendoza (2018 data) is distributed in the following way: Luján de Cuyo (23.4%), San Carlos (15.1%), Tunuyán (13.6%), Tupungato (11.7%) and Maipú (10.9%).

IN 2018, THE SURFACE AREA PLANTED WITH MALBEC IN ARGENTINA HAD REACHED A TOTAL OF 42,999 HECTARES (106,253 ACRES), OF WHICH MENDOZA ACCOUNTED FOR 85.1%: 36,586 HA. BETWEEN 2009 AND 2018 PLANTINGS OF MALBEC IN ARGENTINA INCREASED BY 50.7%.

MAP OF THE LEADING GEOGRAPHIC INDICATIONS OF MENDOZA

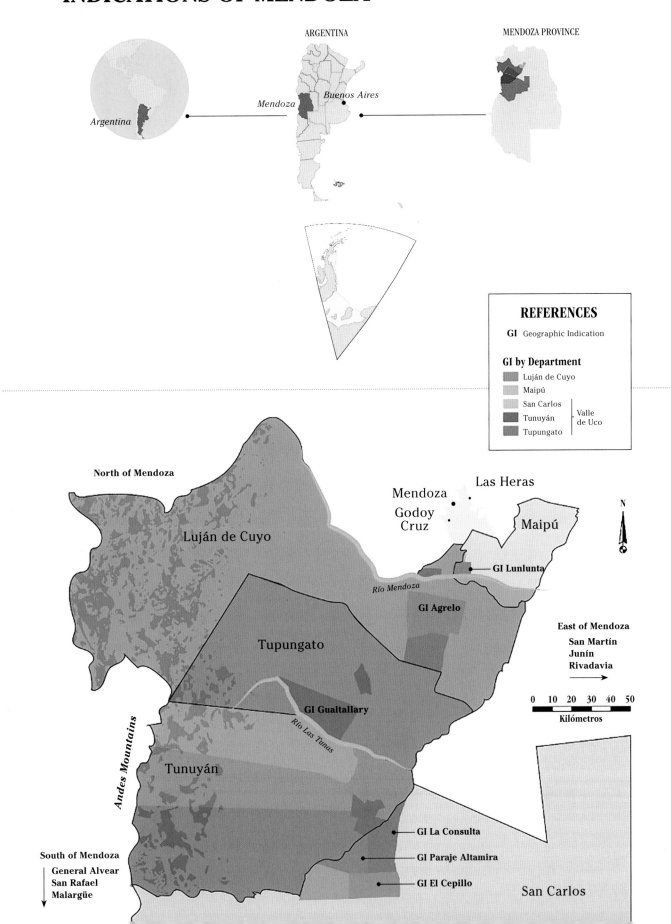

ARGENTINA

MENDOZA PROVINCE

Argentina

Mendoza

Buenos Aires

REFERENCES

GI Geographic Indication

GI by Department

Luján de Cuyo

Maipú

San Carlos — Valle de Uco

Tunuyán — Valle de Uco

Tupungato — Valle de Uco

North of Mendoza

Luján de Cuyo

Mendoza

Godoy Cruz

Las Heras

Maipú

GI Lunlunta

Río Mendoza

GI Agrelo

Tupungato

East of Mendoza
San Martín
Junín
Rivadavia
→

GI Gualtallary

Río Las Tunas

Tunuyán

Andes Mountains

0 10 20 30 40 50
Kilómetros

GI La Consulta

GI Paraje Altamira

GI El Cepillo

San Carlos

N

South of Mendoza

General Alvear
San Rafael
Malargüe
↓

VITICULTURE —

↓   ↓

Sustainable   ## Organic

Sustainable viticulture is a cultivation method that seeks to preserve the biodiversity of a vineyard through natural means. It encourages the use of natural cover crops in between the vine rows as a way to provide shelter for beneficial birds and insects. Cover crops and surrounding native forests shelter species that naturally regulate the ecosystem, reducing the amount of agro-chemicals needed to keep the vineyard healthy and productive. Sustainable farming favors the use of mechanical techniques for weed control rather than herbicides. It involves reducing the use of finite natural resources such as water and energy, and caring specially for the people who work in the vineyards. Sustainability as a system aspires to leave the planet in the same state that we found it. It involves reducing wine's carbon footprint in myriad ways: by lowering the weight of glass bottles, for example, and employing re-usable and recyclable supplies that have a low environmental impact. In helping to conserve the planet, sustainable wineries and companies focus on measuring the environmental and social impact .... of their production processes. Sustainability as a way of life seeks to balance low environmental impact with profitability, which is ultimately necessary to keep the product and value chain sustainable over time.

Viticulture biologique, as it is known in France, forbids the use of synthetic fertilizers and pesticides, replacing them with certified organic products. Similarly to sustainable viticulture, organic farming aims to improve soil fertility by natural methods. The level of nitrogen (vine food) in the soil is augmented through the use of natural compost and guano and through cover crops such as legumes, which naturally increase the amount of nitrogen in the soil. A commonly used antifungal and antimicrobial product that has caused some controversy in organic viticulture is Bordeaux Mixture, or *bouillie bordelaise*, which contains ········· copper sulfate. Although it's allowed in organic farming, this product can be very damaging to the microorganisms in the soil. In rainy areas where it is applied multiple times a year, it can even have a negative effect on the ecosystem. In Argentina, organic viticulture tends to be kinder to the environment. Much credit goes to the dry mountain climate, which helps keep vines naturally healthy.

→ Biodynamic

First conceived in the 19th century and inspired by the ideology of Austrian philosopher Rudolf Steiner, biodynamic agriculture seeks to achieve a balance between plants, the planet and the cosmos. Vineyard activities are coordinated according to the phases of the moon and the stars. The theory is that nature is in balance with the heavens and biodynamic practices ensure that equilibrium is maintained between the vineyard and its natural environment. The vineyard is given homeopathic doses of materials derived from dead animals and insects, and preparations of chamomile and ground silica are applied with the goal of increasing fertility and biodiversity. Biodynamic certifications exist, but many producers simply practice the philosophy without obtaining certification. Biodynamic practitioners claim that their wines are more authentic because of their special methods. For a vineyard to obtain biodynamic certification it must follow organic practices, which include, for example, the use of Bordeaux mixture, permitted to prevent peronospora, a fungal disease that develops after heavy rain.

THE CLIMATE OF
MENDOZA

A general overview of the climate of Mendoza

The Andes act as a barrier against the humid winds of the Pacific, which is why the climate of Mendoza is primarily influenced by the 620 miles that separate it from the Atlantic Ocean. Over 90% of Mendoza's surface area receives around 200 mm (8 inches) of rainfall a year, mostly in summer.

The climate in the wine-growing regions of Mendoza varies according to altitude and latitude. For every 330-foot rise in elevation, the temperature drops by an average of about 1°C, creating a number of very different micro-climates—ranging from Winkler Zone I to Winkler Zone IV— within very small distances. The degree-days (or accumulated heat) of a certain area are calculated by adding up the average daily temperatures above 10°C (the temperature threshold at which a plant starts to develop) between October 1st and April 30th, for the Southern Hemisphere, and between April 1st and October 31st for the Northern Hemisphere.

The Winkler Index and the micro-climates of Mendoza

The accumulated heat metric used by the Winkler Index is calculated adding the monthly average of temperatures above 10°C (50°F) and expressed in degree-days. Region I encompasses those areas with fewer degree-days than 1,389, while Region V encompasses all the warmer regions with degree days above 2,222. The Winkler Index has been used throughout every wine-growing region in the world, and although it has been subjected to local refinement and critique, it continues to be widely used.

Accumulated rainfall (mm/year)

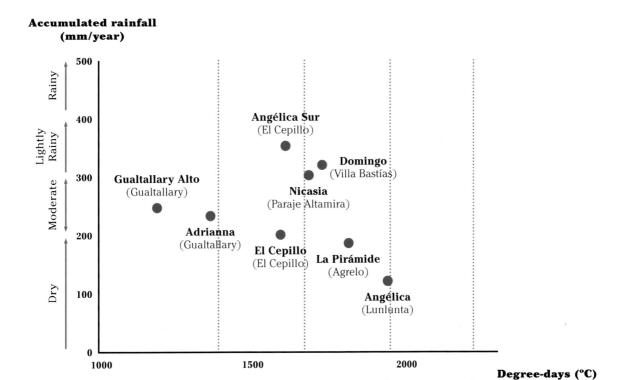

Diagram showing the rainfall and degree-days at each of the Catena Family's vineyards for the 2018-2019 cycle.

THE WINKLER INDEX WAS CREATED IN 1944 BY DOCTORS AMERINE AND WINKLER. THESE TWO FAMOUS UC DAVIS PROFESSORS USED TEMPERATURE DATA FOR THE SEVEN MONTHS FROM BUDDING TO THE LOSS OF LEAVES IN FALL TO DEFINE CALIFORNIA'S VINEYARD-SUITABLE REGIONS. THE INDEX THEN SPREAD WIDELY TO OTHER WINE-GROWING PARTS OF THE WORLD.

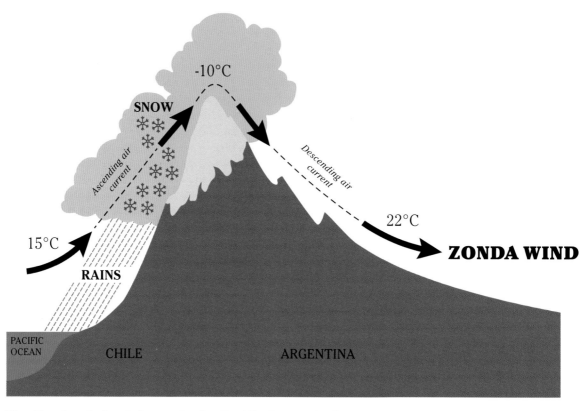

The Zonda wind originates in the Pacific Ocean. It rises up over the Andes and sheds humidity over the Chilean side. Later, as it travels down the eastern Andean slopes onto the Argentine side, Zonda becomes a warm and dry wind.

Climatic difficulties for Mendoza vineyards

Zonda. During autumn, winter and early spring, Mendoza, San Juan, the south of La Rioja and the north of Neuquén are regularly hit by a regional wind: the Zonda. If the Zonda occurs while the vines are blooming, it may lead to a reduction in yields.

Hail. Another adversity faced by Mendoza wine growers is hail, which generally falls toward the end of spring or in early summer. Hail is made up of ice balls that vary between 5 and 50 mm (0.2 to 2 inches) in diameter and can easily destroy a vineyard's entire production. A hail cloud, which takes on the shape of a lemon ice cream swirl, forms when a column of warm, damp air rises above the freezing level (the altitude in which the temperature is at 0°C).

Frosts. Frost is defined as an agrometeorological event that occurs when temperatures below 0°C provoke damage to a vineyard. In Mendoza, frosts most commonly occur in spring, when the amount of heat lost by the soil during the night is greater than the caloric input from the sun during the day. This kind of frost typically occurs under clear skies, when there is little wind and humidity is low.

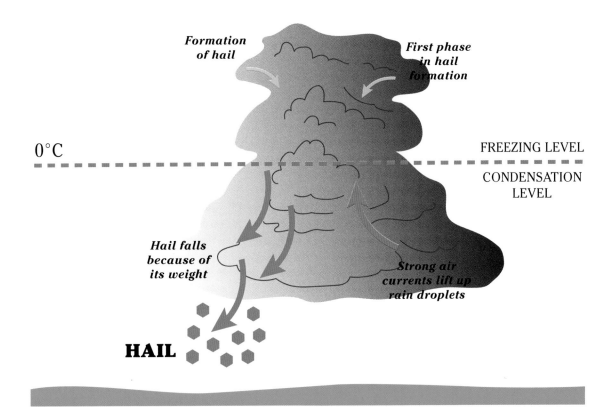

Formation
of hail

First phase
in hail
formation

0°C

FREEZING LEVEL

CONDENSATION
LEVEL

Hail falls
because of
its weight

Strong air
currents lift up
rain droplets

HAIL

Hail occurs when a column of warm, damp air rises up above the condensation level.

AN EFFECTIVE METHOD OF PREVENTING
DAMAGE BY HAILSTORMS CONSISTS OF
PLACING A THICK POLYETHYLENE MESH
OR HAIL NETTING OVER THE VINES.
DEPENDING ON HOW IT IS PLACED, HAIL
NETTING CAN ALSO HAVE AN EFFECT ON
HOW MUCH SUNLIGHT REACHES THE
GRAPE CLUSTERS. IF THE MATERIAL USED
IS BLACK, FOR EXAMPLE, IT MIGHT REDUCE
THE AMOUNT OF LIGHT THAT REACHES
THE PLANT BY UP TO 17%.

Spring frost at La Pirámide vineyard.

The importance of irrigation water

Mendoza's scarce rainfall is unable to meet the water needs of all of its vineyards; extra water must be provided by the vine grower. Irrigation is necessary for the survival of the region's vines. "Crops could not exist without farmers; if not for human activity, this would still be a large desert with vegetation solely on the banks of natural sources of water," says Alejandro Vigil. "The Huarpe people of the Inca Empire who used to live in Cuyo, as documented in pre-Hispanic records, knew that to develop agriculture they needed to channel the Andean glacier water and use it efficiently for watering. This was how they managed to grow crops and survive in such inhospitable terrain. Why am I talking about this? Basically because when we grow a vineyard, we produce drastic and almost irreversible changes on the land." And what influence do humans have on a viticultural *terroir*? "So much influence that

we have changed the behavior of a climber into a plant that actually vegetates [grows] for six months and sleeps for another six," Alejandro insists. "So, when we talk about *terroir*, what we are talking about is how a specific human culture transforms a place over time, using the resources of climate and soil, and not the other way around. In the future, I think this definition of *terroir* will become the accepted one, when we finally acknowledge that wine only exists because humans exist. And this is the truest identity of wine, this dear beverage used to alleviate sorrow and open hearts."

Laura objects to Alejandro's definition of *terroir* as primarily a human construct. "This climber that is the vine survives in poor soils and inhospitable places where other crops can't grow," she says. "Yes, indeed, without humans the vine might not have found these places to grow, these extreme climates where it thrives; and yes, it is true that without human interference

Images of a Scholander Pressure Chamber, which is used to measure the plant's water potential.

the vine would grow wild. But there is a limit to what human intervention can achieve. There is nothing that a human can do to get a *grand cru* out of a soil that is too fertile or too hot."

Alejandro Vigil adds: "We can define *terroir* as the centenary human experience of cultivating a certain place and making its wines."

IN MENDOZA SUBTERRANEAN WATER CAN BE FOUND BETWEEN A DEPTH OF 260 TO 660 FEET. WITH AN AVERAGE RAINFALL OF 200 MM (8 INCHES) PER YEAR, MENDOZA IS WITHOUT DOUBT A DESERT.

In most of Europe's qualitative wine regions, irrigation is forbidden. In the old days, if a winemaker wanted to "cheat" and increase his yields, he would water in secret. The wine producers who established laws of *Appellation d'origine contrôlée* were quite right to forbid irrigation in Bordeaux. The water table in Saint-Émilion, for example, is at a depth of between 2 and 40 feet, so the vine almost always has access to water, and rainfall is about 900 mm (36 inches) per year. In Mendoza, on the other hand, the water table is generally between 260 and 660 feet deep, an impossible depth for the roots to access. Studies show that vines raised to produce high-quality wine require a moderate level of water stress between fruit set and verasion. Extreme water stress is not recommended, however. If the vine is over-stressed under hot summer conditions, it will close its stomata and stop photosynthesis. In Mendoza, where rainfall averages 200 mm (8 inches) per year, the vine would simply die without irrigation, which is why glacier

Photographs of flood irrigation at the Angélica Vineyard. Flood irrigation is the traditional watering method in Mendoza's vineyards; it is being replaced by drip irrigation for qualitative and sustainable reasons.

water (essentially pure mineral water) is used judiciously, imitating rainfall patterns; watering is stopped after flowering and then used only when necessary to restore a vine's equilibrium.

"LEARNING HOW TO PROPERLY WATER THE VINES REQUIRES YEARS OF TRAINING. IT TAKES A MIX OF EXPERIENCE, INSTINCT AND SCIENCE." LAURA CATENA

Today a tool known as the "Scholander Chamber," or "Pressure Chamber," is used to assess the plant's water potential. This instrument measures the water status of a plant by placing a leaf and stalk in a chamber and applying pressure with gas. The higher the pressure required to obtain sap from the stem, the lower the plant's water potential.

In general, the traditional method of watering in Mendoza consists of supplying the soil with all the water it can retain prior to budbreak. This method mimics what happens in viticultural regions where heavy rains occur mostly in winter. During spring the water consumed by the vine can be gradually replaced. Then in summer the vines can be watered more or less, depending on the strategy for the vineyard—being mindful that the plant needs to stop its vegetative growth to concentrate on producing polyphenols,

In recent decades, drip irrigation has expanded in Mendoza, allowing for more precise and sustainable water management.
Photo: Sara Mathews

a key component of wine quality. It is important to note that the Scholander Chamber is simply a complement to the viticulturist's eye. Nothing beats the experienced viticulturalist's years of experience and visual memory of a particular vineyard and its parcels in guiding watering decisions throughout the entire vegetative cycle.

The effect of low temperatures

Cool temperatures allow the grapes to conserve natural acids, enhancing aging potential. Additionally, cooler temperatures enable the grapes to retain anthocyanins (color molecules) and important aromatic compounds.

"TAKING CARE OF THE LITTLE DETAILS IN THE VINEYARD IS PROBABLY THE MOST IMPORTANT FACTOR IN PRODUCING QUALITY WINE."
ALEJANDRO VIGIL

A MAJOR ADVANTAGE OF VITICULTURE IN MENDOZA IS THAT VINES ARE WATERED BY MOUNTAIN RIVERS ORIGINATING IN THE ANDEAN GLACIERS—WHICH MEANS OUR VINEYARDS "DRINK" MINERAL WATER, WATER RICH IN NUTRIENTS, WATER CLEANED BY MOUNTAIN STONES, WATER FREE OF CONTAMINANTS AND POLLUTANTS. TODAY, HOWEVER, WE ARE FACED WITH A WATER EMERGENCY CREATED BY CLIMATE CHANGE. IN THE LAST TWENTY YEARS, GLOBAL WARMING HAS CAUSED THE ANDEAN GLACIERS TO MELT AND SHRINK IN SIZE.

Traditional flood irrigation wastes a great deal of water and can result in excessive yields (and poorer quality) because it is not easily adjusted to different soils. Clay soils, for example, retain more water than stony ones. This is why sustainably farmed vineyards apply drip irrigation. But it often takes years to learn how to manage irrigation in order to draw out the best wine quality from a given parcel. Irrigation in Mendoza is more art than science. It's not a matter of just watering on certain days of the week. Experienced viticulturists study the clouds and the mountains and use their visual memory from years on the job to discern when to water and when to hold back. *How much* to water is decided by walking the vineyards and looking at the vines. The Scholander Chamber can also be used to measure the water needs of every plant—but a veteran vine grower is an essential resource for those seeking to improve the quality of the wines produced by each plant and parcel within a vineyard.

EASTERN
MENDOZA

In Eastern Mendoza, life is slow and traditional. Delimited by the rivers Mendoza (to the north) and Tunuyán (to the south) and located east of Mendoza City, this is one of the most historic regions in the province; it was the most relevant place for viticulture before the rise of the Uco Valley. The lower altitude (below 2,700 feet) makes it a warmer area. The deep and permeable soils are home to large numbers of pergola (or parral) plantings, an elevated trellis system that protects the vines and grapes from heat and frost. Only in Eastern Mendoza will you find old Bonarda vines. The region's blend of Bonarda and Malbec yields easy-drinking wines with vivid color and ripe flavors.

The origin of Eastern Mendoza's soils

During the Pleistocene Era, large masses of detritus (fragments of broken rock) were transported by glaciers and rivers from deep in the Andes to the eastern valleys. Great amounts of water from mountain rivers carried a tremendous mixture of rocks of different origins, ages and sizes. The Tulumaya River, active during this period, was blocked in the late Pleistocene era by the progressive rise of the Lunlunta Sierras. This led to the formation of the paleo-river (old river) Zonda, which carried all the materials from the Andes across the sierras to the east and northeast of the province. Finally, in the Holocene Era, the rise of the Lunlunta Sierras created a split in the Paleo-River Zonda to form the current rivers Mendoza (to the north) and Tunuyán (to the south). Subsequent geologic events gave rise to fluvial (formed by rivers), lacustrine (formed by lakes) and aeolian (formed by wind) deposits.

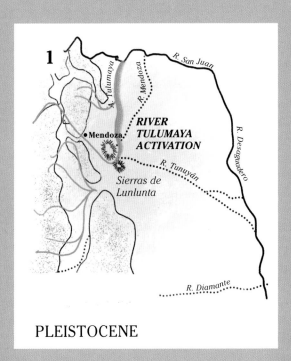

1

A. Tulumaya
R. Mendoza
R. San Juan
RIVER TULUMAYA ACTIVATION
Mendoza
R. Desaguadero
R. Tunuyán
Sierras de Lunlunta
R. Diamante

PLEISTOCENE

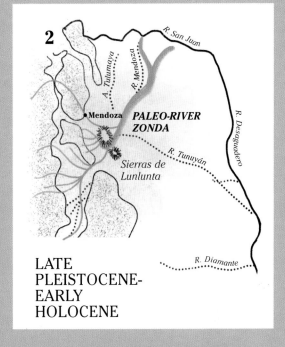

2

A. Tulumaya
R. Mendoza
R. San Juan
PALEO-RIVER ZONDA
Mendoza
R. Desaguadero
R. Tunuyán
Sierras de Lunlunta
R. Diamante

LATE PLEISTOCENE-EARLY HOLOCENE

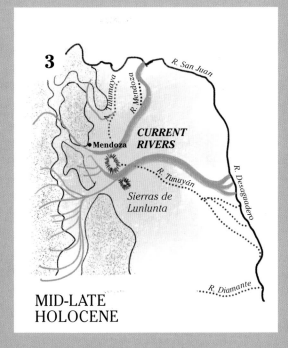

3

A. Tulumaya
R. Mendoza
R. San Juan
CURRENT RIVERS
Mendoza
R. Desaguadero
R. Tunuyán
Sierras de Lunlunta
R. Diamante

MID-LATE HOLOCENE

DEVELOPMENT OF THE PALEO-RIVER ZONDA INTO THE TWO CURRENT RIVERS: MENDOZA AND TUNUYÁN.

ERA	PERIOD	EPOCH	IN MILLIONS OF YEARS
Cenozoic (Age of Mammals)	Quaternary	Holocene	0.01
		Pleistocene	1.8
	Tertiary	Pliocene	5.3
		Miocene	23.0
		Oligocene	33.9
		Eocene	55.8
		Paleocene	65.5
Mesozoic (Age of Reptiles)	Cretaceous		145
	Jurassic		200
	Triassic		251
Paleozoic	Permian		299
	Carboniferous		359
	Devonian		416
	Silurian		444
	Ordovician		488
	Cambrian		542

Geological eras from the Paleozoic to the Cenozoic.

Fluvial deposits

During the Pleistocene and Holocene periods, a high-energy flow of water from west to east gave rise to a sequence of fine alluvial deposits that became interspersed with coarse conglomerates, river stones and gravels of many sizes, reflecting what the rivers carried on their way to the lakes.

Lacustrine deposits

During the Holocene period, deposits of fine materials—silts and clays—and the presence of gastropods (fossils) in the Barrancas area all the way to the farthest part of the Tunuyán river alluvial fan, indicate a lacustrine environment.

Aeolian deposits

The late Holocene is characterized by aeolian sediments (deposited by wind) which suggest for this period a much drier climate, probably similar to our climate today. This aeolian activity may also indicate a significant reduction in the frequency and size of floods. The northward displacement of the Mendoza River most likely occurred during the 18th century in the late

Holocene. The continuing rise of the Lunlunta sierras and the resulting reduction in water flow toward the end of the 17th century would have decreased the size of the area's rivers and streams. This was the most significant climatic change of that time. While the eastern sector of Mendoza's provincial capital continued to flood, the area around Barrancas, to the south, grew much drier, with lower seasonal water flow. The water level of the Mendoza River continued to decrease, and although a few significant flooding events occurred in the 19th century, none were reported thereafter.

Soil texture

The soils of Eastern Mendoza are predominantly sandy loam in texture mixed with gravels and river stones in the higher areas (2,500-foot elevation), and sandy-silt mixed with clay in the lower areas (2,100-foot elevation). These generally deep and permeable soils are low in organic content and overall fertility. Some sectors are not suitable for agriculture because of their salinity.

LUNLUNTA

Lunlunta is located in the Department of Maipú within the "Primera Zona." The so-called "First Zone" also includes Luján de Cuyo, a traditional winemaking region with a large number of high-quality vineyards.

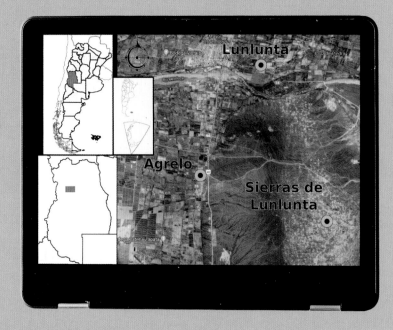

Location of Lunlunta, Agrelo and the Lunlunta Sierras.

The geological origins of Lunlunta have much in common with those of Eastern Mendoza. The Lunlunta area was also influenced by the migration of the paleo-rivers (about 3 million years ago) and the progressive rise of the sierras (about 10,000 years ago). But Lunlunta's proximity to the Mendoza River alluvial fan (Maipú Cone) and to the Lunlunta Sierras resulted in very specific and distinctive conditions.

Large quantities of water with detritus (broken-up rock), generated by rapid summer storms in the southwest of the Lunlunta Sierras, led to the formation of deep river canyons (up to 70 feet deep). Unlike Eastern Mendoza, Lunlunta did not suffer from significant flooding; the main influence on its soil formation came from the migration of the rivers and subsequent eolic deposits brought by wind. Lunlunta's soils are marked by terraces and conglomerates. Conglomerates are a type of sediment that forms when different rocks and minerals (greater than 2 mm in size) become cemented together, often within a fine matrix of carbonates. As a result, the soil surface is fairly heterogeneous.

Angélica Vineyard

The Angélica Vineyard is located in Lunlunta and was named after Dr. Nicolás Catena's mother. Planted between 1920 and 1930, it is home to the Catena family's oldest Malbec vines and is the source of the Catena Cuttings, the largest and most diverse *massal* selection of Malbec plants in the world and the foundational project of the Catena Institute in 1995. The vineyard is located on the northern edge of the Mendoza River, at 3035 f.a.s.l., where river-bed erosion has made the vines appear as if they might fall into the river (see photo on p. 102). In its oldest sections, the Angélica Vineyard continues to be watered through flood irrigation in the traditional manner, in spite of the fact that switching to drip irrigation would be more sustainable. Using drip irrigation could cause the death of this historic vineyard, so the Catena family have chosen to maintain traditional flood irrigation. The vineyard has heterogeneous soils that form into terraces to the north. Textures range from loamy silt to loamy sand in the southern sector where the vineyard meets the river. In some parts of the vineyard we find deep layers of calcium carbonate (limestone) and rounded stones in very loose soil.

Angélica Vineyard in Lunlunta

Laura Catena in the Angélica Vineyard going over the annual climate report.

Old Malbec
vine

Soil profiles in the Angélica Vineyard, Lunlunta

Profile 1
Topsoil with loam and loamy silt textures; looser textures below 30–40 cm (12–16 inches). This profile is present in the northern and northeastern sectors of the vineyard.

Profile 2
Loose soil texture: sandy to loamy-sand soil found in the sectors closest to the Mendoza River. Scattered layers of calcium carbonate.

Profile 3
Round river stones and gravels in layers. Found throughout the vineyard in specific parcels.

Profile 1

Profile 2

Profile 3

The Lunlunta Sierras.

DESCRIPTORS FOUND IN MALBECS FROM MAIPÚ, MORE SPECIFICALLY FROM LUNLUNTA:

smoky

oak

(even in wines that aren't barrel-aged)

strawberry

citrus

(grapefruit, lemon)

cherry

SWEETNESS IS A DESCRIPTOR THAT APPEARS IN MOST WINES FROM THIS AREA*

*Sensory analysis conducted at the Catena Institute.

Climate

Historic temperature records present an average annual temperature of 16°C (60.8°F) and an annual thermal amplitude (night-day temperature difference) of around 13.5°C. The Angélica Vineyard mostly falls into Zone IV (warm) on the Winkler Scale as it accumulates 2,288 degree-days (historic average). On cooler years it falls into Zone III (warm-temperate). Rainfall is similar to the average in the City of Mendoza, which is about 215 mm (8.5 inches) per year.

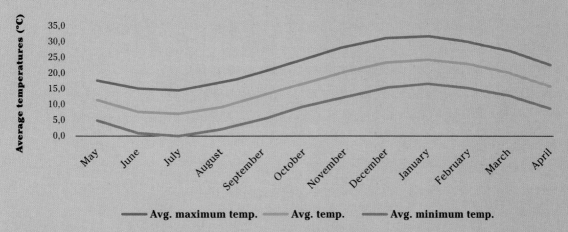

Temperatures in the Angélica Vineyard

Average monthly temperatures for the Angélica Vineyard according to 26 years of data from the vineyard's weather station.

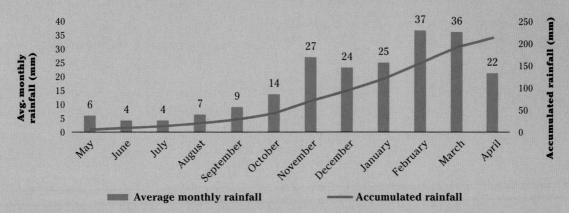

Precipitations in the Angélica Vineyard

Monthly and accumulated rainfall at the Angélica Vineyard according to 21 years of data from the vineyard's weather station.

AGRELO

Located to the south of the Mendoza River between the Andes and the Lunlunta Sierras, Agrelo is near the apex of the Mendoza River alluvial fan at an altitude of around 3,100 feet above sea level.

Geological history

The origins of the soils of Agrelo are closely related to the processes described for Eastern Mendoza and Lunlunta with regards to the migration of the rivers and the progressive rise of the Lunlunta Sierras. The fact that Agrelo is located at the apex of the Mendoza River alluvial fan might suggest that the soil materials would be larger in size than those farther down the alluvion in Maipú and Eastern Mendoza. But Agrelo has its own particular geological history, marked by water and flooding. During the late Pleistocene and early Holocene, large volumes of water flowing down from the Andes mountains were interrupted by the rise of the Lunlunta Sierras. This caused flooding over the entire region and deposits of light materials such as clay and silt—not the gravels one might expect to see at the origin of an alluvial fan. The Andean snowmelt continued to feed this lacustrine setting up until the late Holocene, when the weather became dry and eolic (wind) deposits slowly transformed the landscape into what it is today.

La Pirámide Vineyard

La Pirámide vineyard was planted in 1982 in Agrelo, Luján de Cuyo, and is located at 3,100 f.a.s.l. in a topographical depression. Cool air tends to stagnate, and when there is humidity, a dense fog can almost completely reduce visibility. The area is also susceptible to hailstorms, which is why many vineyards are protected by hail netting. Soils are rich in clay, which lends freshness and moisture to the vines and grape clusters in summer.

The Catena Cuttings collection (pre-phylloxera Malbec clones) originally sourced from the Angélica Vineyard have been replanted here at La Pirámide, four per row, under similar soil and climate conditions and cultivated in exactly the same way, allowing us to study their viticultural and oenological profiles.

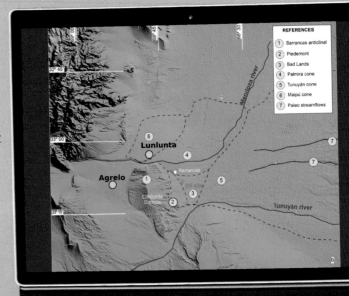

Location of Agrelo at the apex of the alluvial fan of the Mendoza River.

**La Pirámide
Vineyard,
Catena Zapata,
Agrelo.**

**A section of
La Pirámide Vineyard
containing over 130
selections of Malbec,
the Catena Cuttings.**

Soils

The soils in Agrelo are a bit heavier than in other areas of Mendoza. On average they contain around 40% silt, 30% sand, 30% clay and 0.8% organic matter.

These soils retain more moisture because of their elevated clay content. Their fine texture of silts and clays makes them more susceptible to salinity and compaction. In winter the salts are "rinsed" with water to ensure a healthy rest for the vine roots. Planting cover crops is essential in improving drainage and nutrient availability in the soil.

Preliminary studies by the Catena Institute have shown that La Pirámide Vineyard is host to a large and diverse population of soil microorganisms.

Clay soil profile at La Pirámide Vineyard.

COVER CROPS REGENERATE NUTRIENTS AND SOIL MICROBIAL ACTIVITY WHILE THE LAND IS FALLOW IN PREPARATION FOR REPLANTING WITH VINES. THE LLAMAS HELP "CUT THE GRASS" AND PROVIDE NATURAL FERTILIZER.

Soil pit at La Pirámide Vineyard in Agrelo.

DESCRIPTORS FOUND IN MALBEC FROM AGRELO:

chocolate

black pepper

leather

wood

nutty

IN THE MOUTH, WINES FROM AGRELO TEND TO HAVE MEDIUM ASTRINGENCY LEVELS, AND IN SOME CASES THE SALINE DESCRIPTOR IS PRESENT*

*Sensory analysis conducted at the Catena Institute.

Climate

Average annual temperature is around 14.8°C (58.6°F) while daily thermal amplitude averages 15.3°C. The sum of degree-days places the vineyard mostly in Zone III of the Winkler Scale and occasionally in Zone IV during hotter seasons. Annual precipitation is around 272 mm (11 inches) per year.

Temperatures at the La Pirámide Vineyard

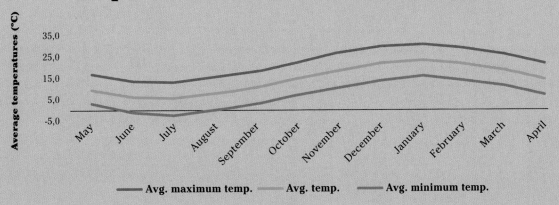

Average monthly temperatures at the La Pirámide Vineyard recorded by the vineyards weather station for the past 26 years.

Rainfall at the La Pirámide Vineyard

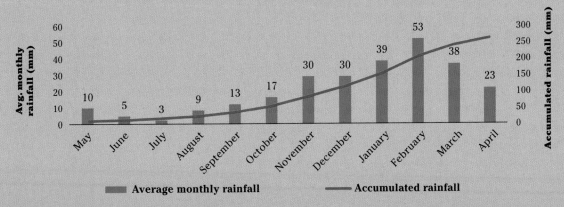

Monthly and accumulated rainfall at the La Pirámide Vineyard according to data from the vineyard's weather station over a 26 year period.

PARAJE
ALTAMIRA

The Paraje Altamira "Indicación Geográfica" (Geographic Indication) is located to the south of the Uco Valley, half a mile southwest of La Consulta in the Department of San Carlos. Historically, the area has long been known for its production of fruits such as apples, pears, peaches, grapes and tomatoes of excellent color with intense flavors and aromas.

Paraje Altamira: view of the Andes. Rocks of alluvial origin covered in calcium carbonate, which makes them appear white.

General geological characteristics

The soil we see today is the result of events that occurred between the early Pleistocene period (about 2 million years ago) and today. The tectonic plates that initially gave rise to the Andes Mountains have continued to move and modify the landscape along with all forms of alluvial, volcanic and eolic activity; the movement, molding and erosion of rocks and minerals over time have given rise to today's geomorphology.

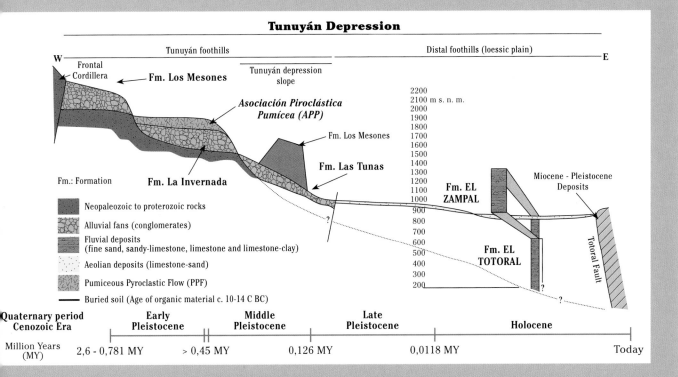

Schematic diagram of the Tunuyán Depression. Geomorphological and lithostratigraphic units presented alongside their related geological eras (Adapted from Mehl, 2011).

The formation of the Tunuyán River and its alluvial fan

The Tunuyán River is one of the largest rivers in Mendoza; its water is used to irrigate most of the Uco Valley. It was formed over many millions of years, creating an enormous alluvial cone as it came down from the Andes. Four glaciations were interspersed with cycles of fluvial erosion, which generated a diversity of mineral deposits such as pumice rock (of volcanic origin) and conglomerates (fragments larger than 2 mm contained within a finer matrix and held together, usually, by calcium carbonate). It is important to note that during the glacial eras, Mendoza was a very humid place. But since the last glaciation, Mendoza has become progressively less humid, turning into the arid region it remains today.

The Paraje Altamira GI "Indicación Geográfica" (in orange and purple) and its location in relation to the alluvial surface of the Tunuyán River (in blue).

Characteristics of the Tunuyán River's alluvial fan

The Tunuyán River's alluvial fan spreads openly from west to east without any interruptions from hill formations (such as we find in Gualtallary). Thanks to the large size of the river and the minimal slope, the cone has a very large surface area. The Tunuyán Cone's materials traveled long distances from their origins in the Principal and Frontal Cordillera and received input from over thirty streams. It's no wonder the rocks from the Principal Cordillera are fragile and degrade easily—their origins trace back to the Mesozoic Era. These ancient rocks come together with limestones and marine sediments (also from the Mesozoic) to form the region's calcium carbonate-rich soils. We also find enormous round white stones in the soils of Paraje Altamira, some up to 2 m (6.5 feet) in size, so big that farmers often use them as barriers between neighboring vineyards. These enormous stones formed either when the glaciers melted at the apex of the cone or through the rupture and collapse of natural dams.

142

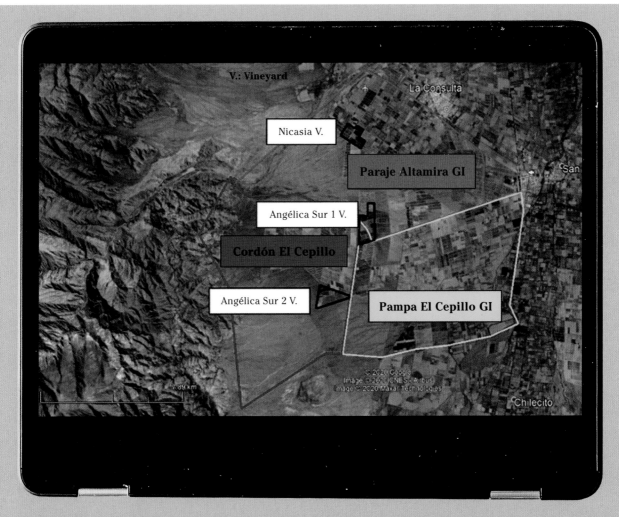

Google Earth map of Paraje Altamira (marked in red). To the south are Pampa El Cepillo and Cordón El Cepillo (marked in yellow and blue). The black outlines indicate the Catena family's three vineyards in the GIs of Paraje Altamira and El Cepillo.

Paraje Altamira becomes an IG, Indicación Geográfica

The outstanding quality of wines coming out of Paraje Altamira led Catena in 2009 to partner with other local producers in order to have the area geologically demarcated and registered as a Geographic Indication. The leading researcher hired for the study was Dr. Stella Maris Moreiras, who holds a PhD in Geology and is a CONICET researcher and a tenured professor in Edaphology at the Faculty of Agrarian Sciences of the Universidad Nacional de Cuyo. In 2013 the Paraje Altamira GI was officially recognized by the National Argentine

BECAUSE OF THE OUTSTANDING QUALITY OF THE GRAPES AND WINES OBTAINED FROM PARAJE ALTAMIRA, IN 2009, CATENA, TOGETHER WITH OTHER PRODUCERS AND DISTINGUISHED RESEARCHERS AT LOCAL INSTITUTIONS, STARTED THE PROCESS OF REGISTERING THE AREA AS AN GI. OFFICIAL CERTIFICATION WAS APPROVED IN 2013, AND IN 2016 PARAJE ALTAMIRA WAS EXPANDED TO ITS CURRENT BORDERS.

225 SOIL PITS INSIDE PARAJE ALTAMIRA AND IN THE IMMEDIATELY SURROUNDING AREAS WERE ANALYZED AND HELPED DEFINE A DISTINCTIVE GEOLOGIC ORIGIN FOR THE GI.

The factors evaluated were soil texture (percentages of sand, silt and clay), calcium carbonate content, and depth at which a physical impediment for the roots was encountered.

Institute of Viticulture and became a national model for asserting the importance and value of the places of origin for local wines. In 2016 Paraje Altamira was expanded to its current boundaries.

The edaphic study (soil analysis)

Satellite images followed by field inspections and edaphic studies allowed us to establish the northern and eastern borders of Paraje Altamira GI. To achieve definitive results, more than 225 soil pits were dug up inside Paraje Altamira and in the immediately surrounding areas.

This allowed for an evaluation of soil texture (percentages of sand, silt and clay), calcareous content and topsoil depth (above the bedrock). Through a Linear Discriminant Analysis (LDA), the eastern and northern boundaries between the Paraje Altamira GI and the La Consulta GI were established using differences between calcareous content and topsoil depth. Overall, the main characteristics of the soils of Paraje Altamira are as follows: the depth of the topsoil varies between 0 and 200 cm (80 inches) and has between 1 and 3 layers, the first being of varying depth—between 0 and 107 cm (42 inches). The soil textures are loamy-sandy to sandy-loamy with

Photograph of a soil pit in Paraje Altamira. Rocky soil with calcium carbonate.

Diagram of soil profile layers up to a depth of 2m (7 feet) in the Altamira area.

varying calcium carbonate content. Finally, once the climate and wine characteristics were also taken into consideration, the Paraje Altamira GI was placed inside the northern fan of the Tunuyán River alluvial cone. And the Tunuyán River itself was established as the western border of Paraje Altamira. To the south, Paraje Altamira is defined by a line that originates in the mountains and transects the Tunuyán River Fan at its midway point. Paraje Altamira has northeast and east exposure, whereas El Cepillo, in the southern part of the Tunuyán Fan, has east and southeast exposure (making it cooler).

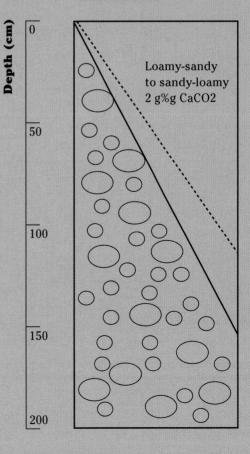

Loamy-sandy to sandy-loamy 2 g%g CaCO2

Nicasia Vineyard in Paraje Altamira Climate Conditions

The Catena family's Nicasia Vineyard is located within the Paraje Altamira GI at 3,600 f.a.s.l. The climate is continental with frequent cold days and nights, significant thermal amplitude, and temperatures as low as 5°C (41°F) on summer nights. The average annual temperature of the vineyard oscillates around 14.6°C (58.3°F), while the annual thermal amplitude is around 15.6°C. Nicasia tends in most seasons to fall in Zone III (warm-temperate) on the Winkler scale (1,743 degree-days). Rainfall is about 320 mm (13 inches) and generally comes in the form of summer storms, when it can rain as much as 60 mm (2.4 inches) in an hour.

Temperatures in the Nicasia Vineyard

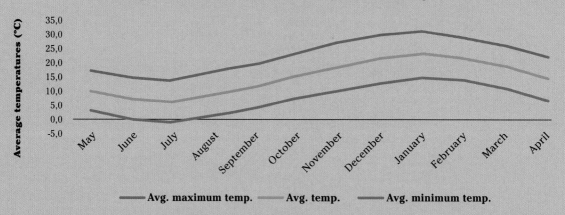

Average monthly temperatures for the Nicasia Vineyard according to 18 years of data from the vineyard's weather station.

Precipitations in the Nicasia Vineyard

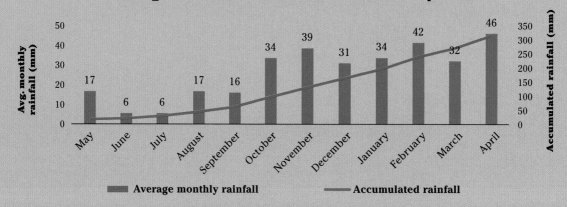

Monthly and accumulated rainfall at the Nicasia Vineyard according to 18 years of data from the vineyard's weather station.

RED WINES FROM THIS AREA PRESENT A HIGH CONCENTRATION OF POLYPHENOLS THAT MAKE THEM VERY DARK WITH EXCELLENT BODY AND STRUCTURE. ANOTHER CHARACTERISTIC IS THE VELVETY NATURE OF THE TANNINS, WHICH MAKES THEM VERY EASY TO DRINK. THANKS TO THE COOL NIGHTS, THE WINES PRESENT A BALANCED ACIDITY THAT CONTRIBUTES FRESHNESS.

AMONG THE SENSORY DESCRIPTORS OF MALBEC FROM PARAJE ALTAMIRA WE FIND:

chocolate

(in all wines tested, even in those not aged in oak)

smoke

citrus

fresh grape

IN THE MOUTH THERE IS A SPICY TACTILE SENSATION*

*Sensory analysis conducted at the Catena Institute.

EL CEPILLO

Dating back to the XVIth Century, El Cepillo is named after one of the first cattle ranches established in the area. In a royal decree of 1575, the Indigenous Peoples' land of Caseopot was granted to Don Domingo Sánchez Chaparro. The Spanish captain founded an estate that he called El Cepillo located in what are now the districts of Eugenio Bustos and Chilecito in the Department of San Carlos. Today the locals know the area south of Paraje Altamira and Eugenio Bustos as El Cepillo (which also means "the brush" in Spanish). El Cepillo is bordered to the east by Highway 40, to the west by the Andes, and to the south by the districts of Tres Esquinas and Chilecito.

The Geographic Indication

The official certifications of Paraje Altamira (to the north of El Indio road) and Pampa El Cepillo (to the south of El Indio road) as Geographic Indications (GI) were the result of concerted efforts by local producers to obtain recognition for the importance of climate and geology in defining a wine terroir. The GI certification indicated on a wine's label helps the wine consumer begin to appreciate (and seek out) the flavors and aromas of each location.

If the label of a Malbec says "Paraje Altamira" or "Pampa El Cepillo," according to the Law of Geographic Indications in Argentina, 100% of its grapes must come from said Geographic Indication.

General characteristics

The topographic altitude of Eugenio Bustos, at the foot of the Andes, varies between 3,200 and 4,600 feet above sea level. The climate is continental with intense cold spells and a wide

TWO GI HAVE BEEN PROPOSED IN EL CEPILLO: THE CORDÓN EL CEPILLO GI AND THE PAMPA EL CEPILLO GI; THE LATTER WAS APPROVED IN 2019.

The Catena family's Angélica Sur Vineyard in El Cepillo.

thermal amplitude.

The alluvial fan of the Tunuyán River (described in the Paraje Altamira section) is at the origin of both Paraje Altamira and El Cepillo Geographic Indications. There are marked differences between the two GIs, however. To the west of El Cepillo we find more ancient soils, dating back to the Pleistocene Era, made up of angular and loosely consolidated colluvial rocks. Slope gradients and orientations differ from those of Paraje Altamira, creating unique micro-climates.

Geological map

From a geomorphological point of view, based on the Q1, Q2 and Q3 alluvial surfaces of the Tunuyán River (see diagram on page 150), the most significant surfaces in the El Cepillo

GI are: alluvial surface Q1, the oldest, and alluvial surface Q3, the most recent, which also includes the Paraje Altamira GI. Q2, in contrast, is smaller and less important.

Pampa El Cepillo GI

The Pampa El Cepillo GI's western border on its Q1 alluvial surface is marked by the Constantini road at an elevation of 3,500 f.a.s.l. To the east, Pampa El Cepillo stretches to Highway 40, encompassing the southern part of the Q3 alluvial surface, which has a south-facing slope and a lower altitude. The smaller Q2 surface is also part of the GI's southern border. The El Retiro road, in the lowest part of the GI and the historic edge of the El Cepillo ranch, completes the southern border of Pampa El Cepillo. The Pampa

149

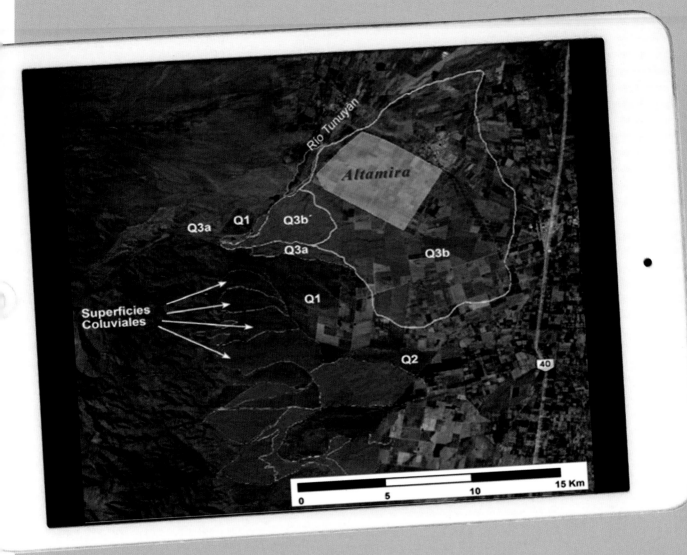

Satellite image showing the alluvial cone of the Tunuyán River with its different surfaces and the colluvial surfaces of El Cepillo.

El Cepillo altitude range is between 3,200 and 3,500 f.a.s.l. Soils are loamy-sand with topsoil depth between 65 and 140 cm (2 and 5 feet) and 1% slope gradients. Average minimum temperatures are lower (colder) than in the Paraje Altamira GI.

Cordón El Cepillo GI

The Cordón El Cepillo GI is located in the Q1 alluvial surface of the Tunuyán River Cone on the western border of Pampa El Cepillo and to the south of Paraje Altamira. It is located between 3,500 and 4,600 f.a.s.l. and has a 6% slope. The soils are sandy to loamy-sandy with a depth of between 140 and 160 cm. The proportion of stones in the soil can be as high as 75%, with large rock fragments and calcium carbonate over some sectors. Colluvial gravels cover the entire surface of the GI and increase towards the west, closer to the mountains. Cordón El Cepillo's southern exposure means average temperatures are even lower

NAME	CORDÓN EL CEPILLO	PAMPA EL CEPILLO
Height	3,500-4,600 f.a.s.l.	3,200-3,500 f.a.s.l.
Geomorphology	Q1	Q3
Soil texture	Sandy and loamy-sandy	Loamy-sandy
Soil depth	140-160 cm	65-140 cm
Slope	6.00%	1.00%
Minimum temperatures	-4 to -6°C	-7 to -10°C
Winkler	III	III
Geomorphology: Dr. Moreiras classified the alluvial cone of the River Tunuyán into three sections defined by their age of formation and characteristics: Q1, Q2 and Q3.		

than Pampa El Cepillo's, but Cordón's greater slope and higher (warmer) minimum temperatures make frosts less likely. A major frost can cause a vineyard's yields to drop significantly and even have a negative effect on the following year's harvest. The Q1 alluvial surface, on which Cordón El Cepillo is located, is different from other sectors of the fan. The significant presence of colluvial gravels on a slope indicates bursts of tectonic shifts and less fluvial influence. In Cordón El Cepillo, one can find Mesozoic marine fossils originating in the Principal Andean Cordillera.

Slope orientation

The map of slope orientations in relation to the geographic north allows us to measure solar exposure and temperature of the soil and atmosphere. Paraje Altamira, with mainly northeast and east-facing slope orientations, is the warmest area, while Pampa El Cepillo, with mainly south/southwest-facing slopes, is cooler. The higher altitude and south-facing slopes of Cordón El Cepillo are even cooler on average. But the downward flow of cool night air coming from Cordón's steeper slopes results in higher minimum temperatures.

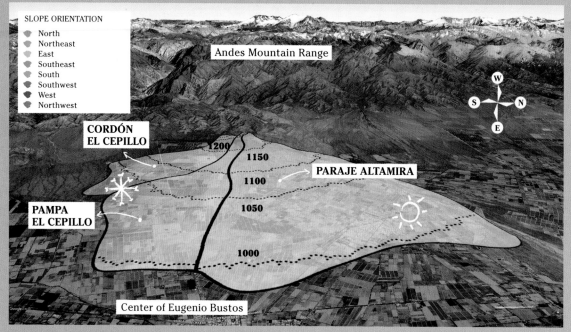

Andes Mountain Range

CORDÓN EL CEPILLO

PARAJE ALTAMIRA

PAMPA EL CEPILLO

1200
1150
1100
1050
1000

Center of Eugenio Bustos

Map of slope orientation

(Elevations in meters above sea level)

Climate characteristics

Precipitation in El Cepillo is twice the provincial average, with around 407 mm (16 inches) annually. Rainfall doesn't fall uniformly throughout the year and is generally associated with violent summer storms. That is why it is important to maintain and protect the natural mountain waterways and irrigation ditches from erosion, especially in the highest-elevation vineyards. El Cepillo has a continental climate with very intense cold spells,

significant night-day temperature differences and low summer nighttime temperatures. Historic records indicate that the average annual temperature is around 13.6°C (56.5°F) and the thermal amplitude is around 16°C. On the Winkler Scale, the Angélica Sur vineyard is located in Zone III with 1,720 degree-days. Advective and radiation frosts, both early and late in the pre-harvest season, are a recurring problem.

Temperatures in the Angélica Sur Vineyard

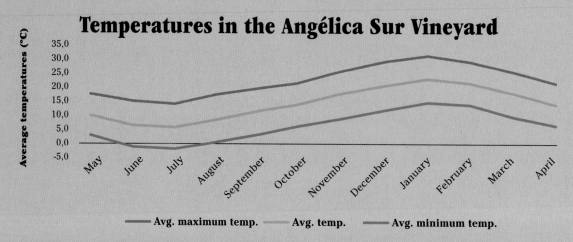

Avg. maximum temp. — Avg. temp. — Avg. minimum temp.

Average monthly temperatures for the Angélica Sur Vineyard according to 8 years of data from the vineyard's weather station. The vineyard is located in both Pampa El Cepillo and Cordón El Cepillo.

MALBEC WINES FROM EL CEPILLO OFFER THE FOLLOWING FLAVORS:*

plum

(a very intense sensory descriptor)

fresh grape

floral aromas

(of medium intensity)

spices

(less intense)

medicinal aromas

(present in some wines)

*Sensory analysis conducted at the Catena Institute.

Precipitations in the Angélica Sur Vineyard

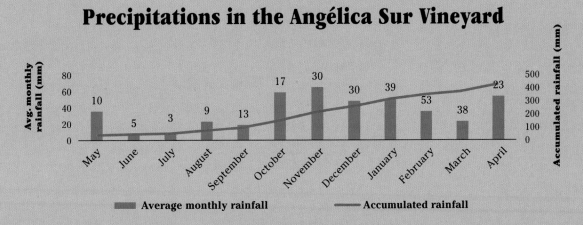

Monthly and accumulated rainfall at the Angélica Sur Vineyard according to 8 years of data from the vineyard's weather station.

GUALTALLARY

The Gualtallary Geographic Indication is on the Las Tunas River alluvial fan. It is a region rich in geologic events.

Satellite image of the Gualtallary district in Tupungato showing that it is part of the Las Tunas River alluvial fan (outlined in red). In blue is the current course of the Las Tunas River. In brown are two series of hills ("lomas") that formed later. The light blue dot represents the location of the Adrianna Vineyard belonging to the Catena Zapata family.

A brief geologic history of Gualtallary

Gualtallary has an average slope of about 3.6% from the beginning of the Las Tunas alluvial cone down to Highway 89 at the edge of the Geographic Indication. In contrast to other regions, in Gualtallary water flowed rapidly through a narrow alluvial fan instead of spreading out into a wide area. The small Las Tunas River deposited stones not much bigger than a soccer ball. A peculiarity of this cone is that a new geologic fault arose after the formation of the Andean Cordillera. This fault, located to the north of the Gualtallary District, gave rise to two chains of hills: Las Lomas del Jaboncillo and Las Lomas de El Peral. When the entire northern part of the Las Tunas alluvial cone rose up, the water moved south and deposited large amounts of calcium carbonate, today one of the most distinctive features of Gualtallary's soils.

Soil layers in Gualtallary

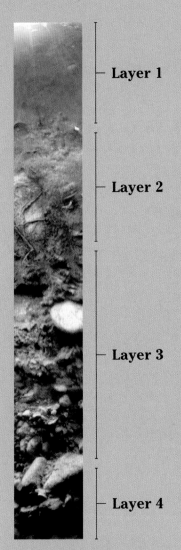

- Layer 1
- Layer 2
- Layer 3
- Layer 4

A complete soil profile in Gualtallary with description of four layers.

Layer 1
Sandy soil. 90% usable soil, 10% rocks (stones smaller than 5 cm in diameter of volcanic origin). Low calcium carbonate content.

Layer 2
Compacted layer, high calcium carbonate content, 88% rocks (plutonic and volcanic stones, limestone and small sand-based gravel). Sandy-loam texture with high percentages of gypsum and calcium carbonate.

Layer 3
Very low volume of usable soil, 8% sand. Stones are coated with calcium carbonate, which gives them a whitish color. Most likely due to leaching of calcium salts from Layer 2. Presence of metamorphic rocks, mainly sedimentary, of plutonic and volcanic origin (granite, diorite, rhyolite, andesite, etc.).

Layer 4
Very low volume of usable soil, 15% sand. Rocks without calcium carbonate coating and minimal calcareous content. Presence of metamorphic rocks, mainly sedimentary, of plutonic and volcanic origin (granite, diorite, rhyolite, andesite, etc.).

ONE OF THE MOST IMPORTANT CHARACTERISTICS OF THE GUALTALLARY REGION IS THE DIVERSITY OF ITS SOILS. THE DEPTH OF EACH LAYER (NUMBERED FROM 1 TO 4, SHALLOWEST TO DEEPEST IN THE DIAGRAM ABOVE), TEXTURE, COMPOSITION AND WATER RETENTION CAPACITY VARY SIGNIFICANTLY WITHIN SHORT DISTANCES.

Above: Alejandro and Laura recreating a scene from "The Addams Family" in a photo shoot with photographer Sara Matthews at the Adrianna Vineyard. Below: Examples of rocks found in Gualtallary.

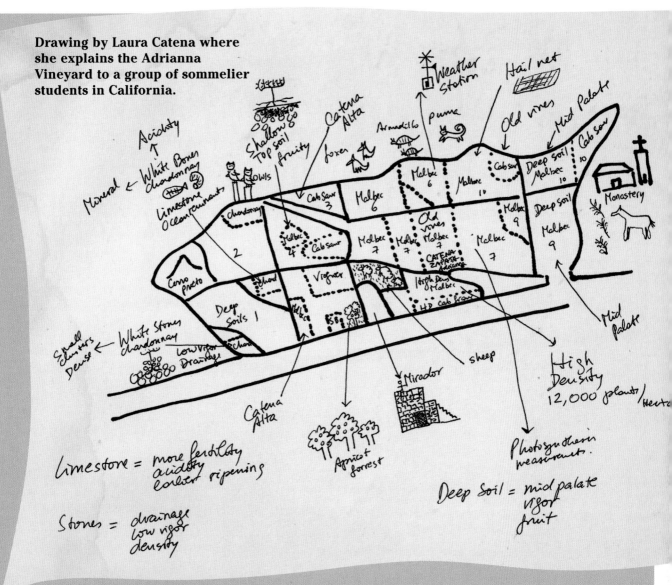

Drawing by Laura Catena where she explains the Adrianna Vineyard to a group of sommelier students in California.

Limestone = more fertility
acidity
earlier ripening

Stones = drainage
low vigor
density

Deep Soil = mid palate
vigor
fruit

The Adrianna Vineyard and its "parcelas"

The Catena family's Adrianna Vineyard is divided into *parcelas* (parcels) according to its different soil compositions. Five of these parcelas have produced world-renowned wines that earned scores of 100 points from wine journalists: the White Stones and White Bones Chardonnays; and the Malbecs: River, Fortuna Terrae and Mundus Bacillus Terrae.

The vineyard is crisscrossed by dry river beds, areas rich in limestone and calcium carbonate and soils of varying depth. A range of elevations, sunlight exposure, slope gradient and orientation result in distinctive and one-of-a-kind characteristics for each parcela.

THE DIVERSITY OF SOILS IN THE ADRIANNA VINEYARD IS RELATED TO LOCALLY OCCURRING PROCESSES IN EACH PARCEL. FOR EXAMPLE, IN SOME SECTORS, WATER WASHED AWAY THE TOP LAYERS AND LEFT SOILS THAT ARE ALMOST ALL STONE ON THE SURFACE. THEN, JUST 30 TO 50 FEET AWAY, YOU MIGHT FIND CALCIUM CARBONATE–RICH LAYERS 15 TO 20 INCHES IN DEPTH, CLOSE TO THE SURFACE; AND JUST ANOTHER 50 TO 100 FEET AWAY THE SOILS MIGHT BE SOMETHING ENTIRELY DIFFERENT.

Soil profiles

1. Calcareous

The soil profiles of the Adrianna Vineyard's Mundus Bacillus Terrae Malbec and White Bones Chardonnay parcelas are similar. The first 50 cm (20 inches) of soil contain a loose loamy-sand or sandy-loam texture. Then comes a layer of limestone that prevents the thicker roots from progressing; only finer roots are found at depth beyond the limestone layer. Finally, there is a layer of rounded stones.

2. Deep

The soil of the Fortuna Terrae parcel contains a very deep layer (deeper than 1.5 m/5 feet) of loamy-sand or sandy-loam. Toward the bottom of the profile we find a layer of rounded stones in addition to the limestone typical of this area.

3. Stony

The stony soil profile of the Adrianna Vineyard's River Malbec and White Stones Chardonnay parcelas is quite similar. As seen in the photograph, stones of different sizes are covered in a fine layer of calcium carbonate. There are also rocks formed by volcanic activity through the process of cooling and warming of minerals and the resulting fluctuations in pressure and temperature. In some cases the rocks are weathered and disaggregated. In this kind of soil, the roots penetrate deeply. Studies by the Catena Institute have shown fine roots at depths greater than 2 m (6.5 feet) below the surface.

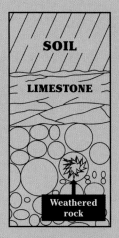

Soil composition in the Mundus Bacillus Terrae parcela. Left: photo of the vineyard soil profile. Right: diagram

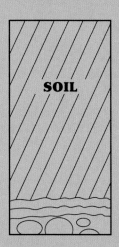

Soil composition in the Fortuna Terrae parcela. Left: photo of the vineyard soil profile. Right: diagram

Soil composition in the River parcela. Left: photo of the vineyard soil profile. Right: diagram.

Example of rocky soil in Gualtallary.

Example of "lasagna"-type soil profile in Gualtallary Alto.

Other soil profiles: Gualtallary Alto at 5100 f.a.s.l.

4. a) "Lasagna" Soil

Gualtallary's diversity of soils can be observed both on the surface while walking the parcelas, and below, where one can see the different ways in which the layers have settled under the ground. On the diagram we see a soil laid out in layers similar to the layers of a lasagna. The top layer has a loose, loamy-sand texture, second are layers of calcium carbonate and stones, and the third is a layer of stones with no calcium carbonate. The final layer is a sector with greater amounts of clay mixed in with small gravels and river sand.

4. b) Fully calcareous soil

In this case, the soil profile begins with 30 cm (12 inches) of calcareous soil and continues with rounded stones covered in calcium carbonate.

Example of calcareous soil in Gualtallary Alto.

Climate

In Mendoza's high-altitude wine region, the average temperature usually decreases by about 1°C for every 100 m (330 feet) increase in altitude. This is why temperatures are quite cool in an extreme high-altitude vineyard (at almost 5,000 feet elevation) such as Adrianna. The average annual temperature in the Adrianna Vineyard is around 12.5°C (54.5°F). It is important to note that because of the natural slope of the region, cold air tends to flow rather than settle, meaning that frosts are rare despite the region's cool climate. Adrianna falls in either Winkler Zone I (cold) or II (temperate), depending on how cold the year is. Rainfall is more plentiful than in lower-altitude areas near Mendoza City, with a historic average of 409 mm (17 inches) per year.

Temperatures at the Adrianna Vineyard

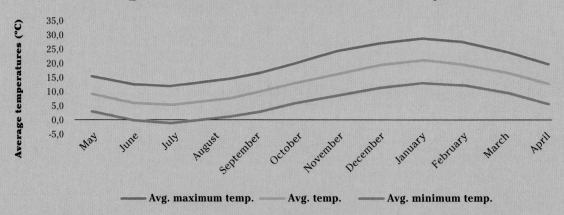

Average monthly temperatures for the Adrianna Vineyard according to 21 years of data from the vineyard's weather station.

Precipitations in the Adrianna Vineyard

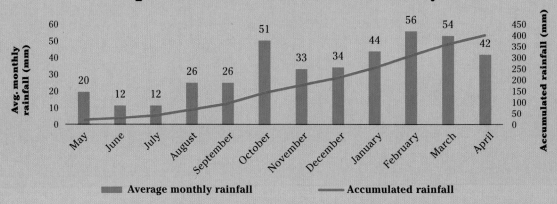

Monthly and accumulated rainfall at the Adrianna Vineyard according to 21 years of data from the vineyard's weather station.

SENSORY ANALYSIS OF MENDOZA MALBEC IN TWENTY-NINE *PARCELAS* (PARCELS) UNDERTAKEN BY THE CATENA INSTITUTE PRODUCED THE MOST EXTENSIVE STUDY OF *TERROIR* FOR ANY WINE VARIETY IN THE WORLD. ACCORDING TO THESE STUDIES, THE SENSORY PROFILE OF GUALTALLARY MALBEC INCLUDES THE FOLLOWING:

floral aromas

spices

eucalyptus

berries

ADRIANNA *PARCELAS*. Some of the descriptors that can be assigned to specific soil types in the vineyard are as follows: stony soils tend to yield astringency, acidity and aromas of mint and alcohol, while deep soils offer pepper, jammy aromas and sweet sensations. Minerality didn't vary statistically between soils although it was a descriptor that the tasting panel found more frequently in shallower soils.*

*Sensory analysis conducted at the Catena Institute.

7

Road trip through the **Uco Valley** and other wine regions

Luis Reginato, Alejandro and Laura at La Pirámide Vineyard.

Laura, Alejandro and Belén Iacono, the agricultural engineer in charge of the Adrianna Vineyard and Catena Director of Sustainability.

Laura at the Great Wall of China with the journalist James Suckling and his wife, Marie.

Alejandro and Laura in the vineyard.

Alejandro in Burgundy with the harvest crew.

Laura, Alejandro and Nicolás tasting *grands vins* in preparation for the assemblage of Nicolás Catena Zapata.

Laura and her father at Bodega Catena Zapata.

Maricel, Nesti, Laura, Lucía and Alejandro, what a team!

Laura and Alejandro at the snow-covered Adrianna Vineyard.

A visit from the famous journalist Jancis Robinson to Gualtallary Alto.

THE ANDES MOUNTAIN RANGE

Cerro Negro
(6152 m)

Cerro Tupungato
(6635 m)

Río Tunuyán

TUPUNGATO

Paraje Altamira

Gualtallary

88

← *To San Rafael*

El Cepillo

40

TUNUYÁN

LA PLATA RANGE

Cerro del Plata
(6075 m)

Lunlunta ■
Agrelo ■

Eastern Mendoza

■ Tupungato

■ Gualtallary

■ Tunuyán

Valle de Uco

Paraje Altamira ■   ■ San Carlos

■ El Cepillo

■ **Mendoza**

■ San Rafael

86

To Mendoza Capital →

40

AGRELO   Lunlunta

Eastern Mendoza

EASTERN MENDOZA

Where we live like in the olden days

Laura Catena: To me, Eastern Mendoza is *The Potato Eaters* and *Starry Night* by Van Gogh. And Vermeer maybe too, because they drink a lot of Malbec in the Netherlands. Perhaps because Queen Máxima is Argentinian.

Alejandro Vigil: I think of rural culture. *The Milkmaid*, maybe. But I like Van Gogh's *Starry Night* too because when you're in the east the sky is always full of stars, completely unpolluted.

LC: Well, then, we'll choose that. What are the wines like?

AV: Medium-bodied and lingering in the mouth. Not much tension but powerful with firm tannins.

LC: Firm but gentle tannins and plenty of fruit. I think of the east as a friendly place.

AV: Medium-bodied, easy to drink, without too much acidity. The tannins aren't dry but they are present; the wines are good with food or on their own.

LC: Right, it's the classic wine of Mendoza. Shall we choose some jazz to represent the east? I know! "What a Wonderful World" by Louis Armstrong: lovely, familiar but not cheesy.

AV:

Imagine being at your grandfather's house, La Vendimia, lying on the grass, drinking a Torrontés and listening to Louis Armstrong. That's it, that's the song.

Louis Armstrong.

Alejandro:

I was thinking about how important Eastern Mendoza is to both of us....You have Casa Vigil there, that wonderful restaurant you set up with your family (when I eat there, my favorite dish is costilla de ternera); and my great-grandmother's home was in Eastern Mendoza, such an important part of our family's history. I always remember eating preserved tomatoes with olive oil at La Tata's house...such a classic Mendoza dish.

Laura

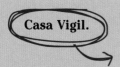

Casa Vigil.

Tata Nicasia's Tomato Recipe:

Boil tomatoes from the garden until the skin is soft. Peel and cut off the ends.

Cut into cubes and mix with sliced onions, whole cloves of garlic, oregano and salt.

Fill sterilized glass jars and cook in a pot for making preserves. Cover with preserve lids and boil for 20 more minutes.

In winter make into a salad with a generous quantity of homemade olive oil and serve with meat or milanesas.

COSTILLA DE TERNERA (BEEF RIBS)
COOKED FOR 12 HOURS AT 80°C (176°F) WITH ROASTED VEGETABLES

First, make a brine in which to soak the ribs for 24 hours—this lends flavor and keeps the ribs moist so they won't dry out while they're cooking for 12 hours. Place enough water in a pan to cover the ribs, three cloves of garlic sliced in half, 1 onion, 1 red pepper and 1 carrot cut into large chunks, salt and pepper to taste, 1 bay leaf, one teaspoon of chili flakes and another of oregano. Bring it to a boil, switch off and let cool. Once the brine is cool, use it to cover the ribs and place in a container in the refrigerator for 24 hours. To start cooking, set the oven at 80°C (176°F), place the ribs on a tray with a little oil underneath and leave in the oven for 12 hours. Next come the roasted vegetables. On another tray coated in olive oil, cut all the vegetables you have into quarters. Add a whole head of garlic and zucchini (cut into quarters) for the final 15 minutes. Season to taste and add olive oil on top before increasing the oven temperature to 180°C (350°F). Remove the foil covering the ribs so they will be brown and crispy when served, and cook the vegetables for about 45 minutes, until they can be pierced easily with a fork

LUNLUNTA

Historic cradle of Mendoza Malbec

40

Laura Catena: I love Lunlunta! Especially when you're going down that little street and around the corner you come across the Nuestra Señora del Tránsito Church, with its brick walls half-covered in ampelopsis (peppervine), which turns red and yellow in winter…

Alejandro Vigil: It's also an area with very old vines and fairly heterogeneous soils. In Lunlunta you have two major terraces: one close to the river and one farther away. The one close to the river has much lighter soils with less clay and silt. The farther you move away from the river, the more clay there is. In 90% of the area, about a meter to a meter and half deep, you find a rocky subsoil filled with round alluvial stones.

LC: Which is why the drainage is good.

AV: There is excellent drainage until you get to the lower part of Lunlunta, where you're in trouble because the vineyard is at the same altitude as the river—meaning that the vine might have access to water two to two and a half meters below. On the other hand, in the higher parts of Lunlunta, the underground water is deeper than 80 m (260 feet).

LC:

I always wonder why many of the world's best vineyards are near rivers. I imagine it's related to the good drainage and to the fact that dried riverbeds contain interesting mineral deposits.

AV: It's two different things: they've got to be close to a river but not at the same level as the river. In fact, the cheapest wines in Burgundy, the *Villages*, are at the bottom where the vines have continuous access to water two meters below the surface (the river drains to the sides). In Germany, for example, the best wines come from vines located on high terraces above the river. In fact, the vineyard soils are composed of materials with good drainage because they were at one time part of the river (alluvial material).

LC: Which is why our Angélica Vineyard in Lunlunta basically has loam and gravel soils with very good drainage.

AV: Exactly.

LC: To me, Lunlunta is red and dark fruit on the nose, red mostly. But what I most like about Lunlunta is the smooth texture of the tannins. I think Lunlunta is very good for light Malbecs…

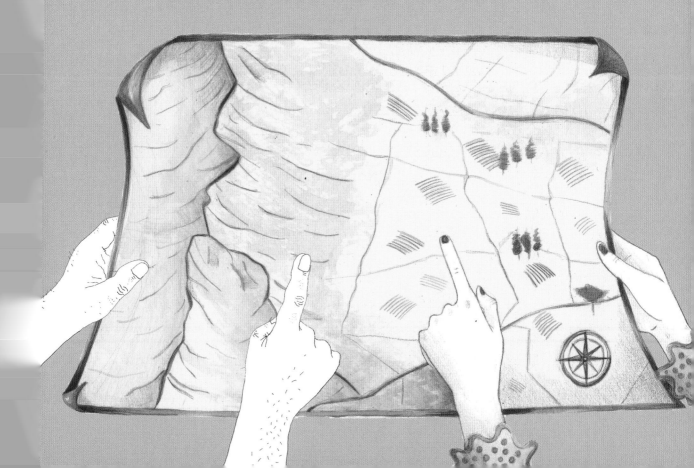

AV: It always makes me think of ripe plums and generous, sweet tannins....Strong wines, delicious wines with power!

LC: Yet, even if the region is warm, I've never felt the wines were too alcoholic.

AV: Obviously, if in Lunlunta you leave the grapes on the vine for too long, you'll get a port. What's interesting to me is maintaining the balance, getting red and dark fruit, volume in the mouth and sweetness without losing the freshness of biting into a plum; first comes the acid, immediately followed by the sweetness.

IF I HAD TO ASSOCIATE A MUSICIAN WITH THE SPIRIT OF LUNLUNTA, IT WOULD BE AMY WINEHOUSE.

LC: Why do you think of Amy Winehouse for Lunlunta?

AV: Because she is hard to define, just like Lunlunta, a land of contrasts. Amy mixed a lot of jazz with elements of rock.

Amy Winehouse.

Illustration inspired by
Las dos Fridas
by Frida Kahlo.

LC: And if Lunlunta were a work of art, what would it be? I was thinking about *Las dos Fridas* by Frida Kahlo, because it represents the connection between the new and the old. Lunlunta is a traditional location with many old vineyards, but the expansion of the city has made it more urban and modern.

AV: Lunlunta could also be that painting by Dali called *The Persistence of Memory*, which mixes time and space.

LC: The one with the drooping clocks? Of course! Dali was so Old World and so contemporary at the same time. Amy Winehouse would have liked to have been paired with him.

AGRELO

86

40

The elite wineries corridor

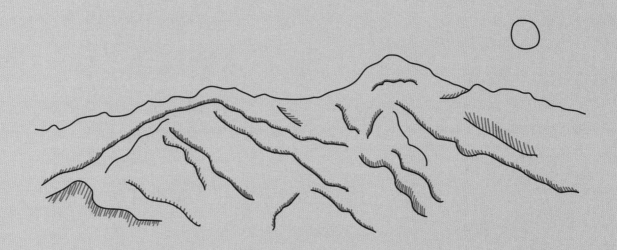

Alejandro Vigil: It doesn't matter how many years I've been coming here…every time I get to Agrelo, I am blown away by the view of the Precordillera.

Laura Catena:

IT'S THE PRIMERA ZONA (FIRST ZONE), BUT IT ALSO REPRESENTS THE REBIRTH OF GREAT ARGENTINE WINE FOR EXPORT. WINERIES SETTLED IN AGRELO BECAUSE THEY SAW IT AS THE CORRIDOR INTO THE UCO VALLEY. AT THAT TIME NOBODY WAS SURE YET THAT THE UCO VALLEY WOULD BECOME THE GOLDEN GOOSE.

When the major wineries set up in Agrelo, Mendoza's producers thought that the best quality would be found there. Most of Mendoza's best-known quality wineries are in Agrelo. It's like the *châteaux de la Loire*, where people went when they wanted to get out of Paris. Like Chacras de Coria, which was a vacation spot and today is a nearby suburb….Only a few years ago Agrelo seemed so far away from Mendoza City!

AV: We've been playing with the idea of associating a place with art and I thought of a painting by Van Gogh, his self-portrait without the beard. The painting could represent Agrelo, yes, because that's what the place is. Agrelo produces very distinctive wine, whether it's Cabernet, Syrah or Malbec: All have a spicy core and remind me of Côte-Rôties from cooler areas….They're not heavy; they're elegant with a chalky texture. Which is what makes me think of a classic painting with very contemporary details. It was the first Van Gogh to be sold at a very high price after he died.

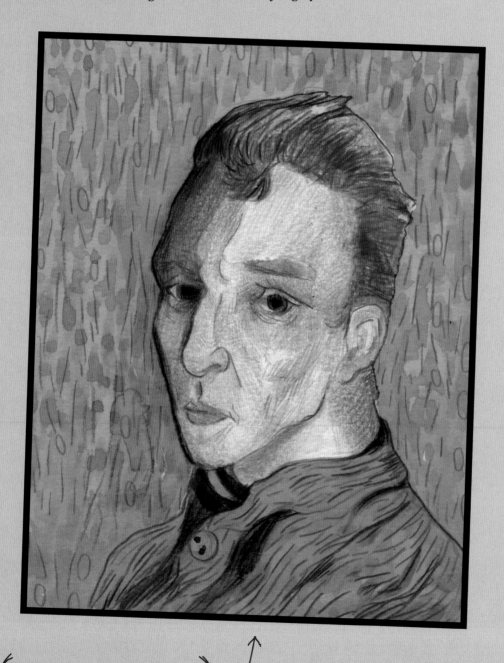

Illustration inspired by
Self-Portrait without a Beard,
by Vincent Van Gogh

LC:

I thought of the Taj Mahal, because with all the historic wineries and the imposing buildings that we find in Agrelo, there is a feeling of being in the midst of something monumental. You know, Ale, when people visit the Catena Zapata pyramid they often tell us there is something spiritual about the place.

And when it comes to music, Agrelo makes me think of Brahms, "Hungarian Dance No. 5"....I love classical music!

AV: I was thinking more of Queen.

LC: We Will Rock You.

Drawing of Catena Zapata's pyramid, by Fernando Maza, an Argentine artist and Laura's uncle.

PARAJE
ALTAMIRA

The white stones kingdom

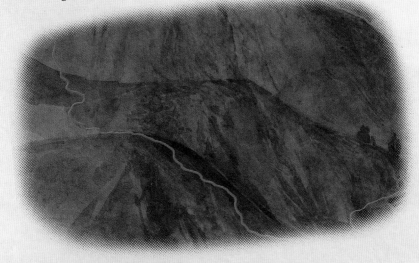

[Stonehenge.]

Alejandro Vigil: Laura, while we tour La Consulta, I have a question to ask: do you think some places are destined to be famous?

Laura Catena: If you're asking about La Consulta, of course! It's producing amazing wines. Especially Paraje Altamira, which has played a role in Argentine history ever since General San Martín rode through on his way to liberate South America. Today everybody is talking about the wines.

AV: Paraje Altamira contains 4,500 hectares (11,000 acres). And a lot of stone.

LC:

Which is why for our "art pairing" I was imagining art made with stones. I thought of Stonehenge, a Japanese Zen garden and Easter Island.

How does it feel,
how does it feel?
To be on your own,
with no direction home.
A complete unknown,
like a rolling stone.

Bob Dylan.

AV: I like Stonehenge. Because Paraje Altamira equals profound wines with weight, ripe dark fruit, violets....I don't see them as austere wines, but rather as powerful. Altamira is *"fuerza"* (strength).

(They listen to Bob Dylan's "Like a Rolling Stone" at top volume).

GETTING THE GEOGRAPHIC INDICATION FOR PARAJE ALTAMIRA CERTIFIED TOOK A LOT OF WORK. SOMEONE HAD REGISTERED THE NAME "ALTAMIRA" BEFORE THE LAW OF 1999, AND THEY WOULDN'T LET PRODUCERS FROM THE AREA USE IT.

LC: We hadn't really worried about it because we could use La Consulta, the Geographic Indication that includes Paraje Altamira, on the label. We never wanted to trademark names of places because that would make us owners of a historic name and prevent other local wineries and small producers from using it. Absurd! It would go entirely against our mission of promoting Argentine wine as a whole. But then we got tired of the Altamira situation and you, Alejandro, and Luis Reginato got to work with other producers from the area. Then came the study we conducted with the Universidad Nacional de Cuyo showing that the alluvial plain of Paraje Altamira had a distinct climate and soil.

After much discussion with the local producers, the INV (National Institute of Viticulture) certified Paraje Altamira as a Geographic Indication in January 2014. It was a battle won by the entire community of Altamira; and lasting bonds were formed among local producers like the Pizzellas, David and Sonia Smith from Finca Alegría, the Zuccardis and Bodega Chandon.

EL CEPILLO

Wild land in the mountain desert

Laura Catena: El Cepillo always makes me think of a remote place, where you feel a little sad and alone but happy because you're in the middle of nature….The way a gaucho (Argentine cowboy) must feel, don't you think?

I remember that time when we were driving down the road, and a group of horses suddenly appeared out of nowhere. I asked you: "What are those horses doing here?" You told me: "They belong to a man who lives over there. He lets them run wild and we keep on telling him to stop, but the horses are still here." El Cepillo is wild, and there is nothing you can do to change that.

In musical terms (choosing a slightly melancholic song that reminds me of the place), I'm thinking of "The Long and Winding Road" by The Beatles (they listen to the song on the smartphone). But when it comes to an artwork to represent El Cepillo—the brand-new Pampa El Cepillo GI, which was certified in 2019—for some reason, gauchos are all that come to mind. Martín Fierro is the quintessential gaucho. Phrases like: "Brothers and sisters be united, this is the first of laws, because if they fight with each other, they are devoured by outsiders." I love these lines. They make me think of you and me as gauchos, cooking an *asadito* on an open fire pit….You'd better be the chef; I'm so bad at cooking! Hold on…we could have a barbecue right here and now, in the vineyard, why not?

And if we're talking about the Malbec from El Cepillo, I think that there is something in these limestone soils, so, so infertile and so well drained, but also uniform in texture, very different from the soils of Gualtallary. And the cold that gets right into your bones, worsened by the chill winds that come from the south, from Patagonia. The wines take on some of that freshness: violet aromas with a lot of spice and blue fruits, but most of all what stands out about the wines of El Cepillo is their structure. I'd say they are among the most tannic of Mendoza's wines, with a solidity that makes them age well and stay forever on the mouth.

Alejandro Vigil:

I VISITED EL CEPILLO A LOT WHEN I WAS A BOY. FOR US KIDS, IT WAS A WILD TERRITORY AT THE EDGE OF CIVILIZATION. WE'D EXPLORE THE DRY RIVER BEDS LOOKING FOR PETRIFIED SHELLS; IT WAS ALL A BIG ADVENTURE.

Today, it's still an adventure. Every time I drive down Highway 40 and head west to San Carlos, on that road that appears stuck to the mountains, it's the spirit of Mendoza that one feels—something very powerful and strong, something to do with nature. So for music I think I will go for a national rock group, from Divididos, something like "El arriero va."

LC: Maybe…

AV: From a visual point of view, to me El Cepillo would be perfectly represented by Kandinsky: the visualization of the object, a mountain with its angular stones. The whole El Cepillo area is made up of slopes in a large alluvial cone, cones within cones. Small dry rivers and their beds, where the material comes from deep inside the Andes, with alluvial soils where glaciers once stood, where the limestones settled and well-drained soils formed. The wines have a potent character, what we might call a "mineral" character: wildflowers, violets, wet stone, cumin, and curry leaf. These are strong wines, wines with an inner life, wines with power but also delicate and subtle. The landscape has two dimensions: cold in the presence of a hugging sun, and stone of the sculpted kind. And all this gives the wine its individual character.

Illustration inspired by
The Sleeping Gypsy
by Henri Rousseau.

LC: What about Klimt? Oh no…you wanted to pair it with Gualtallary! We could pair El Cepillo with Rousseau and *The Sleeping Gypsy*, which has mountains and a woman with a guitar and a lion, reminding us of the limits of cultivation, of the edge of civilization. I love that painting by Rousseau.

AV: I was thinking of associating El Cepillo with something crazy like the film *2001: A Space Odyssey*.

LC: Oh yes, the film begins with "Carmina Burana", which always makes me think of El Cepillo, and the movie does too.

2001:
A Space
Odyssey

GUALTALLARY

From impossible place for viticulture to Grand Cru

Laura Catena: I look at the Tupungato landscapes, especially Gualtallary, such a remote, almost inhospitable place where there is constant threat of frost and the soils are poor and heterogeneous —I can't help but wonder what my father saw when he decided to plant vines here.

Alejandro Vigil:

Nicolás was a visionary, he knew that a place as distinctive and unique as Gualtallary might have, at simple view, poor soils; but this "poverty" of soils that generated just the right amount of stress for the vines would become the secret ingredient for the one-of-a-kind and unforgettable wines of Adrianna. So perhaps, these poor soils were rich after all.

Illustration inspired by
The Kiss **by Gustav Klimt.**

LC: It's a good thing that he trusted his instincts, because this region has produced and continues to produce wines that are unique in South America and beyond.

AV: If the region were a work of art, there's no doubt that it would be *The Kiss* by Klimt.

LC: I was thinking of *The Garden of Earthly Delights* by Hieronymus Bosch, because of its complexity and how it parallels the different soils of Gualtallary. We have both chosen paintings with a great deal of color and power. Which is why for the music I thought of the Russian Dance from *The Nutcracker*.

Kurt Cobain.

AV: The Russian Dance you think? Hmmm…let's find it on Spotify.

LC: The Russian Dance makes me think of Tupungato, of nature. It has energy, tension and harmony all at the same time.

AV: I'd have gone in a different direction, something like Kusturica.

LC: And what do you think of "Smells Like Teen Spirit" by Nirvana? (they listen to it)

(Then they listen to the Russian Dance again.)

LC: Actually, I think that Nirvana wins because compared with Malbec's two-thousand-year history, Gualtallary, at just twenty-five, is a young viticultural region.

AV: Gualtallary is the only place where I detect real minerals in the flavor profile. They're wines with tension, not so fruity or woody. These are naked wines, austere wines. In some cases they have a little red or black fruit like cherries. I'd almost say they have a Pinot Noir profile.

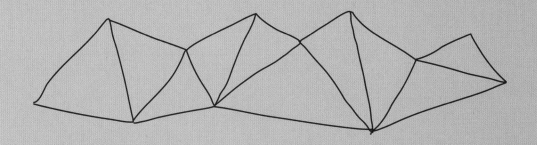

LC:

I THINK OF THEM AS ANGULAR WINES. GUALTALLARY IS LIKE A SKINNY PERSON WHO'S VERY STRONG. A SVELTE WOMAN WITH WELL-DEFINED MUSCLES AND A BIG PERSONALITY.

Villa Bastías (near Gualtallary, in Tupungato) is a little more generous because it has all those stones on the surface that reflect the sunlight onto the grape clusters and lend a certain creamy, buttery feel to the wines.

AV: In terms of music, Villa Bastías would be more pop, more rounded with sweeter endings.

LC: Right, Villa Bastías and Gualtallary are very different. It's like comparing Meursault to Chablis.

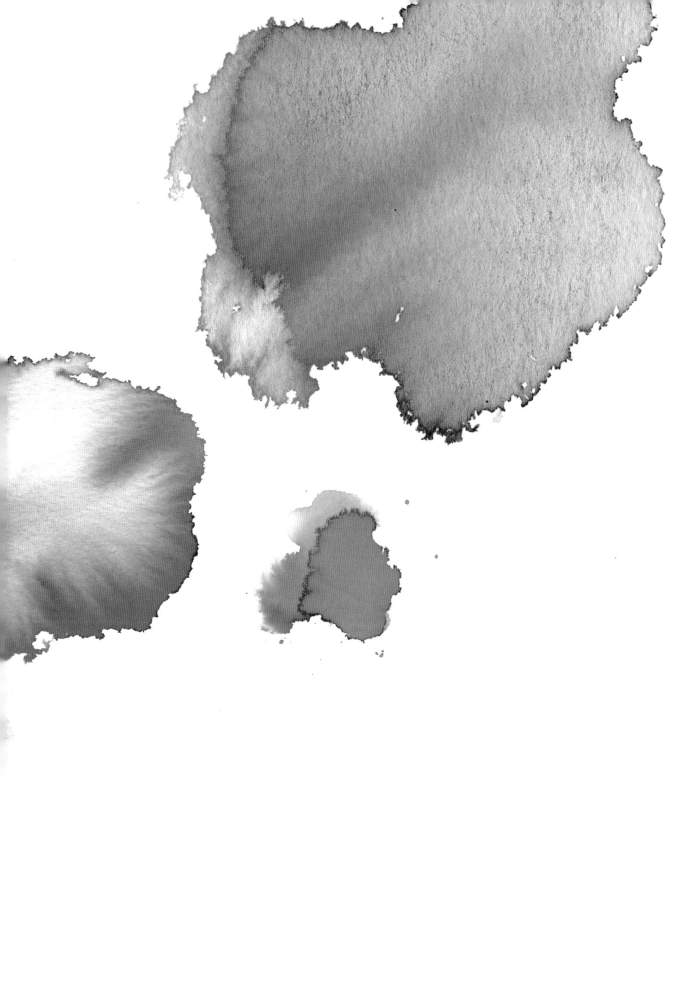

Bibliography

Amerine, M. y Winkler A. (1944). *Composition and Quality of Musts and Wines of California Grapes.* Hilgardia, 15: 493-675.

Araujo, V. S. Frisicale, M.C. Sánchez, N. Turienzo, M. Lebinson F. y Dimieri, L.V. (2019). *The relationship between Cenozoic shallow igneous bodies and Thrust systems of the mountain front of the Cordillera Principal, Mendoza province, Argentina.* Journal of South American Earth Sciences. 92, 531-551. Doi: doi.org/10.1016/j.jsames.2019.03.027

Beezley, William H.: *Malbec Matters,* University of Calgary.
Downloaded from: https://larc.ucalgary.ca/news/malbec-matters

Berli, F. D'Angelo, J. Cavagnaro, B. Bottini, R. Wuilloud, R. y Silva, M. F. (2008). "Phenolic composition in grape (Vitis vinifera L. cv. Malbec) ripened with different solar UV-B radiation levels by capillary zone electrophoresis". *Journal of Agricultural and Food Chemistry,* 56(9), 2892-2898.

Bettiga, L. J. (2003). *Wine grape varieties in California* (Vol. 3419). UCANR Publications.

Boursiquot, J. M. Lacombe, T. Laucou, V. Julliard, S. Perrin, F. X. Lanier, N. Legrand, D. Meredith, C. y This, P. (2009). Parentage of Merlot and related winegrape cultivars of southwestern France: discovery of the missing link. *Australian Journal of Grape and Wine Research,* 15(2), 144-155.

Cara, L. Pérez Valenzuela, R. y Mastrantonio, L. (2016). *Indicación Geográfica de Gualtallary, Mendoza, Argentina.* Facultad de Ciencias Agrarias, Universidad Nacional de Cuyo.

Catena, Laura (2011). *Vino Argentino, An Insider's Guide to the Wines and Wine Country of Argentina,* Cap. 2: Malbec, el vino negro, Ed. Catapulta. pp. 16-42.

Chambouleyron, J. (2005). *Riego y drenaje: técnicas para el desarrollo de una agricultura regadía sustentable.* Tomo I. p. 470. EDIUNC.

Clancy, Tomas. *Eleanor of Aquitaine, teenage queen of France and the rise fall and rise again of Malbec.*
Downloaded from: https://tomasclancy.wordpress.com/2011/06/07/eleanor-of-aquitaine-teenage-queen-of-france-and-the-rise-fall-and-rise-again-of-malbec/

Cohen, K.M. Finney, S.C. Gibbard, P.L. y Fan, J. X. (2013; updated) *The ICS International Chronostratigraphic Chart.* Episode 36: 199-204. Recuperado desde: www.stratigraphy.org/ICSchart/ChronostratChart2019-05.pdf

Colombo, F. (2005). Abanicos aluviales cuaternarios. Andes Argentinos. Geogaceta, 38, 103-106.

Corona, G. (2019). *La geografía del vino. Un estudio sobre el Valle de Uco.* Triñanes Gráfica. p. 183.

D'Armailhacq, Armand (1867). *De la culture des vignes. De la vinification et des vins dans le Médoc avec un état des vignobles d'apres leur réputation,* Bordeaux, P. Chaumas Editor, 3er. Ed.

Departamento de Estadística y Estudios de Mercado. Subgerencia de Estadística y Asuntos Técnicos Internacionales. (2019). Informe de Variedad Malbec. Instituto Nacional de Vitivinicultura.

Dixon, D. y Bernor, R.L. (1992). *The practical geologist.* Fireside. Simon & Schuster Inc. 160 p.

Encyclopaedia Britannica - 9th edition - 1875 to 1889 - vol 24 page 604-605

Fayolle, E. Follain, S. Marchal, P. Chéry, P. y Colin, F. (2019). Identification of environmental factors controlling wine quality: A case study in Saint-Emilion Grand Cru appellation, France. Science of the Total Environment 694 (133718), 1-13.

Gascón, M. (2009). "Recursos para la frontera araucana: Santiago de Chile y Mendoza en el siglo XVII". *Revista TEFROS,* 7, 1-2.

Grande Encyclopédie Française (quote de 1886): sitio web: «ENCYCLOPÉDIE FRANÇAISE», Encyclopædia Universalis [en ligne], consulté le 12 mars 2020. URL: https://www.universalis.fr/encyclopedie/encyclopedie-francaise/

Griset, Pascal y Laborie, Léonard (2016). *Introduction. De qui, de quoi, malbec est-il le nom ?" / "Whom and What is Malbec About?" / "¿De qué, de quién es el nombre malbec",* RIVAR Vol. 3 No 7, ISSN 0719-4994, IDEA-USACH, Santiago de Chile, pp. 1-10.

Jones, G. V. Duff, A. A. Hall, A. y Myers, J.W. (2010). *Spatial analysis of climate in winegrape growing regions in the western United States.* Am. J. Enol. Vitic., 61:313-326.

Lacoste, Pablo (2015). El Malbec de Francia: la denominación de origen controlada "Cahors". Historia y perspectivas. Volumen 33, N° 1. Páginas 113-124 IDESIA (Chile).

Lacoste, Pablo: *Historia del Malbec, cepa insignia de Argentina.* Downloaded from Wines of Argentina web site:
http://www.winesofargentina.org/estadisticas/es/Historia_del_Malbec_por_Pablo_Lacoste.pdf

Lawless, H. T. y Heymann, H. (2010). Sensory Evaluation of Food: Principles and Practices. 473–478. Published by Springer.

Magen, Adolphe (1868). *La Vigne dans le bordelais, Bordeaux,* Imprimerie Centrale de Ve. Lanefranque et fils.

Mehl, A. E. (2011). *Sucesiones aluviales del Pleistoceno tardío-Holoceno, Valle de Uco (provincia de Mendoza): Inferencias paleoambientales y paleoclimáticas.* Tesis presentada para optar al grado de doctor en Ciencias Naturales. Universidad Nacional de La Plata. Facultad de Ciencias Naturales y Museo. Argentina.

Moreiras, S. Erik, M. Hugo, N. Diego, E. y Durán, V. (2013). "Holocene geomorphology, tectonics and archaeology in Barrancas, arid Central Andes piedmont (33°S)", *Applied Geography,* 42, 217-226.

Moreiras, S. y Mastrantonio, L. (2013). *Indicación Geográfica Altamira. Informe Parte 1: Características geográficas, geológicas & geomorfológicas.* Cátedra de Edafología, Facultad de Ciencias Agrarias, Universidad Nacional de Cuyo, 41 p.

Morgan, H.H. Du Toit, M. y Setati M. E. (2017). *The Grapevine and Wine Microbiome: Insights from High-Throughput Amplicon Sequencing. Frontiers in microbiology.* 8:820, 1-15. Doi: doi.org/10.3389/fmicb.2017.00820

Mount, Ian (2012). *The Vineyard at the End of the World: Maverick Winemakers and the Rebirth of Malbec,* W.W. Norton & Company; Illustrated Ed., USA.

Odart, Alexandre-Pierre (1841). *Essai d'ampélographie ou description des cepages les plus estimés*, Tours, France.

Pereyra, F. X. (2019). *Geology and Geomorphology*. Rubio, G. Lavado, R. S. Pereyra, F. X. (Eds.). "The Soils of Argentina". Springer International Publishing AG. World Soil Book Series. 2:7-25. Doi: doi.org/10.1007/978-3-319-76853-3_2

Perez Valenzuela, B. R. Maffei, J. A. y Mastrantonio, L. E. (2012). *Indicación Geográfica Altamira. Parte II: Suelos*. Cátedra de Edafología, Facultad de Ciencias Agrarias, Universidad Nacional de Cuyo, 18 p.

Pisciotta, A. Abruzzo, F. Santangelo, T. Barbagallo, M. G. y Di Lorenzo, R. (2017). *Berries variability: causes and effects on the quality of' Cabernet Sauvignon*. International Symposium on Flowering, Fruit Set and Alternate Bearing. 1229 (201-208).

Ramos, V. A. y Aleman, A. (2000). *Tectonic Evolution of The Andes*. Cordani, U. G. Milani, E. J. Thomas Filho, A. y Campos, A. D. (Eds.). "Tectonic Evolution of South America". Río de Janeiro, 635-685.

Ramos, V. A. y Folguera, A. (2011). "Payenia volcanic province in the Southern Andes: An appraisal of an exceptional Quaternary tectonic setting". *Journal of Volcanology and Geothermal Research*, 201, 53-64.

Rapport de M. Chevreul (1846). *Ampélographie, ou traité des cepages les plus estimés*, Paris, Mme. Bouchard-Huzard Ed.

Rodríguez, José G.; Matus, Mirta S.; Catania, Carlos D. y Avagnina de Del Monte, Silvia. (1999). Caracterización ampelográfica de la variedad Malbec, cultivada en Mendoza (Argentina) según el método de la O.I.V. Publicado en Revista de la Facultad de Ciencias Agrarias (Vol. 31, no. 2) Universidad Nacional de Cuyo. Facultad de Ciencias Agrarias. Centro Coordinador de Ediciones Académicas

Rondon, M. R. Goodman, R. M. y Handelsman, J. (1999). "The earth's bounty: assessing and accessing the soil microbial diversity." *Trends in Biotechnology*. CellPress. 17:403-409.

Salomon, M. Bottini, R. De Souza Filho, G. Cohen, A. Moreno, D. Gil, M. y Piccoli, P. (2013). *Bacteria isolated from roots and rhizosphere of Vitis vinifera retard water losses, induce abscisic acid accumulation and synthesis of defense-related terpenes in in vitro cultured grapevine*. Physiol. Plant. 151, 359–374.

Scacco, A. Verzera, A. Lanza, C. M. Sparacio, A. Genna, G. Raimondi, S. Tripodi, G. y Dima, G. (2010). *Influence of soil salinity on sensory characteristics and volatile aroma compounds of Nero d'Avola wine*. American journal of enology and viticulture, 61(4), 498-505. doi: 10.5344/ajev.2010.10003.

Sweet, Nancy (2012). *Malbec and Cot: From France to Fps*, Foundation Plant Services, FPS Grape Program Newsletter.

Thudichum, John Louis William y Dupré, August (1872). *A treatise on the origin, nature, and varieties of wine: a complete manual of viticulture and enology*, MacMillan & Co., London and New York.

Vallone, R. y Olmedo, F. (2015). *Estudio de ampliación IG Paraje Altamira*. Estación Experimental Agropecuaria (EEA) INTA Mendoza. 50 p.

Van Leeuwen, C. Roby, J-P. y De Rességuier, L. (2018). *Soil-related terroir factors: a review*. Oeno One 52 (2), 173-188.

Williams, G. (1969). *Characteristics and origin of a Precambrian pediment*. J. Geology. 77, 183-207.

Zárate, M. Mehl, A. E. (2019). *Soils of the Cuyo Region*. Rubio, G. Lavado, R. S. Pereyra, F. X. (Eds.). "The Soils of Argentina". Springer International Publishing AG. World Soil Book Series. 9:135-148. Doi: doi.org/10.1016/j.jsames.2019.03.027

Zarraonaindia, I. Owens, S. M. Weisenhorn, P. West, K. Hampton-Marcell. J. Lax, S. Bokulich, N. A. Mills, D. A. Martin, G. Taghavi, S. Van Der Lelie, D. y Gilbert, A. (2015). *The Soil Microbiome Influences Grapevine-Associated Microbiota*. Bio. 6, 1–10.

Research projects by the Catena Institute

Cara, L. (2019). "Informe de la geología y geomorfología de los distritos de Agrelo y Lunlunta en los departamentos de Luján de Cuyo y Maipú". Bodega Catena Zapata.

Mezzatesta, Berli, Buscema & Piccoli (2020). *Impacto del suelo en el crecimiento, rendimiento y calidad de bayas y vinos de V. vinifera L. cv. Malbec en un viñedo comercial de altura*. (Tesis doctoral no publicada). Programa de Posgrado en Biología (FCA - FCM, UNCuyo – CCT). IBAM, CIW. Mendoza.

Pérez Valenzuela, R. (2009). "Relevamiento edáfico de Lunlunta y Agrelo". Bodega Catena Zapata.

Pérez Valenzuela, R. (2013). "Caracterización del *terroir* El Cepillo". Bodega Catena Zapata.

Pérez Valenzuela, R. Mezzatesta, D. Iácono, B. y Reginato, L. (2015). "Informe de los suelos de Gualtallary". Bodega Catena Zapata.

Urvieta, R., Jones, G., Buscema, F. et al. Discriminación de terruño y añada de vinos Malbec basado en la composición fenólica en múltiples sitios en Mendoza, Argentina. Sci Rep 11, 2863 (2021). www.nature.com/articles/s41598-021-82306-0

Urvieta, R. A. (2020). *Caracterización química y sensorial de vinos Malbec. Huella dactilar del Malbec en distintos "terroir" de Mendoza*. (Tesis doctoral no publicada). Programa de Posgrado en Ciencias Agropecuarias (FAUBA-UBA). IBAM, CIW. Mendoza.

Urvieta, R. Buscema, F. Bottini, R. Coste, B. y Fontana, A. (2018). *Phenolic and sensory profiles discriminate geographical indications for Malbec wines from different regions of Mendoza, Argentina. Food Chemistry, 265*, 120–127. https://doi.org/10.1016/j.foodchem.2018.05.083

Collaborators

Luis Reginato, Belén Iácono, Pablo Virgillito, Fernando Buscema, Alejandro Viggiani, Flavia Sosa, Laura Abbruzzese, Roy Urvieta, Ornella Scattareggia, Daniela Mezzatesta, Rodrigo Alonso, Mariano García and Roberto Bolorinos.

The illustrations in this book were made by Martina Trach and Júlia Barata.

Martina Trach: pp. 11, 12, 14, 20-21, 24, 25, 29, 30, 34, 42, 44, 46, 47, 53, 54, 71, 73, 76, 105, 122, 166, 171, 173, 174, 176, 178, 179, 181 (arriba), 183, 185, 186, 187, 190. Tapa.

Júlia Barata: pp. 17, 18, 19, 32, 41, 45, 48, 49, 54, 56, 58, 59, 62, 64, 74-75, 77, 122, 123, 166, 167, 171, 172, 174, 178, 182, 183, 184, 187, 190. Tapa.

Fernando Maza: p. 177; p. 4-5: OldBookIllustration.com

p. 37: Wikimedia Commons, 1874 Popular Science Monthly Volume 5 (autor desconocido)

p. 181: (abajo) 2001-A-Space-Odyssey-1968-UK-Quad-Film-Poster

---

Image Credits

All the images featured in this book came courtesy of the Catena Zapata photographic archive and the following people:

p. 12: Sara Remington; p. 20: Laura Catena in Cahors; p. 22: Shoot; p. 23: Comparative leaf; p. 60: Sara Remington (barrels); p. 61: Lucio Boschi (grapes); p. 65: La Marchigiana Label (Catena family); p. 66: Photos by the Catena family; p. 67: Photos by the Catena family; p. 72: Saint Felicien Wine; p. 80: Pablo Monton (Adrianna Vineyard at night); p. 82-83: Sara Remington (vineyard leaves); p. 84-85: Sara Remington (mountain); p. 86-87: Lucio Boschi; p. 89: Horacio Paone (La Pirámide vineyard); p. 91: Nacho Gaffuri (finding gold in the trench); p. 102: Mercedes de la Vega (Lunlunta bank, Deep Soil); p. 103: Catena Institute (left: stony soil profile; stones and roots); p. 104: spider photo; p. 105: Sara Remigton (bee), Mercedes de la Vega (vicia sativa), Lizzy Butler (owl); p. 108: Horacio Paone (cultivated soil); pp. 110, 111: Catena Institute (sustainability); p. 116: Catena Institute (La Pirámide vineyard); p. 117: Catena Institute, Scholander Chamber p. 118: Pablo Monton; p. 119: Sara Matthews; p. 121: Sara Remington; p. 127: Sara Remington; p. 129: Lucio Boschi (photo Laura Catena); p. 130: Old vine in profile; p. 131: (left: Mercedes de la Vega, Lunlunta, deep soil; right above and right below: Ramiro Pérez Valenzuela); p. 132: Lunlunta landscape (profile, Mercedes de la Vega); p. 135: Sara Remington; Mercedes de la Vega (below); Catena Institute (above, center); p. 136: Mercedes de la Vega (Agrelo, deep soil); p. 137: Catena Institute (La Pirámide in flames); p. 138: Mercedes de la Vega (general, deep soil); p. 140: center: Mercedes de la Vega; right, left: Catena Institute; p. 145: Mercedes de la Vega (Paraje Altamira, stony soil); p. 149: Mercedes de la Vega (Cordón El Cepillo, vineyard landscape); p. 155: Ramiro Pérez Valenzuela; p. 156: Sara Matthews (Alejandro Vigil and Laura Catena in the trench); Mercedes de la Vega (stones); p. 158: Credit Catena Institute (above, center, below); Catena Institute; p. 159: Crédito Catena Institute (above left, above right, below); Catena Institute; p. 168: Instagram @casavigil

With the exception of:

iStockphoto:
p.16: Paper texture © ke77kz; pp. 20, 31: Paper texture © Antonel; p. 22: Grape © kaanates; p. 23: Vine leaf © skydie; pp. 30-31: Dawn at the vineyard © Esperanza33; p.p. 33, 181: Crumpled white paper © NikolaVukojevic; p. 48: Blue sea © piola666 pp. 60, 67: Postage stamp © hudiemm

Unsplash:
p. 13: Green grape © Keegan Houser, purple grape © Nacho Domínguez Argenta, purple grape © Maja Petric; p. 57: Paper texture © Ivan Gromov; p. 66: Photo frame © Chance Anderson; pp. 76, 77, 78, 79: Abstract painting © Pawel Czerwinski; pp. 78-79: Telephone © Quino Al; p. 84: Moon © Neven Krcmarek; pp. 103, 131, 159 (above right, below): Polaroids © Iwan Shimko; p. 105: Butterfly © Daniel Klein; p. 111: Mountain with moon © Benjamin Voros; p. 121: Television © Julian O'hayon; pp. 127, 135 (below), 145, 165: Photo frame © Nauman Abdul Hafeez; pp. 128, 151: Tablet © Brooke Lark; pp. 129, 150: Cell phone © Benjaminrobyn Jespersen; pp. 132, 138, 159 (above left); 164, 168 (center): Photo frame © Ian T; p. 134: Laptop © Dean Pugh; p. 135 (above); p. 135, 140, 164, 165: Photo negatives © Markus Spiske; p. 141: Tablet © Infralist. com; p. 154: Cell phone © Rahul Chakraborty; p.157: Paper texture © Annie Spratt; pp. 166, 174, 182: Paper © Markus Spiske; p.168: Old paper © Annie Spratt; pp. 170, 178, 184: Paper © Annie Spratt; pp. 119, 108: Polaroid © Adrien Olichon.

Miscellaneous:
p. 84: NASA/GSFC/Solar Dynamics Observatory (Sol). www.jpl.nasa.gov/imagepolicy; p. 105: Wikimedia Commons. Micrococcus (CDC/Dr. Richard Facklam –PHIL #977–, 1980), Pseudomonas (This media comes from the Centers for Disease Control and Prevention's Public Health Image Library –PHIL–, with identification number #10043. CDC/ Janice Haney Carr); p. 105: Wikimedia Commons. Pseudomonas (Permission –Reusing this file–. PDUSGov-HHS-CDC); p. 105: Wikimedia Commons. Azospirillum brasilense was isolated from the city of Derna Libya. 30 November 1899. Source: Own work; p.105: Wikimedia Commons, Bacillus cereus, SEM image. Mogana Das Murtey and Patchamuthu Ramasamy.

From the graphics:
pp. 106, 109: Catena Institute; p. 113: Harvest Report Catena Zapata; p. 128: Cara, 2019; p. 134: Moreiras, et al., 2013, pp. 147, 158: Catena Institute; pp. 164, 165, 166, 170, 174, 174, 178, 182, 186: José País; p. 157: Laura Catena; pp. 141, 150, 151, 154: Luis Reginato; p. 107: Roy Urvieta; p. 107: Ornella Scattareggia; p. 97: Adapted from Ramos & Folguera, 2011, pp. 99: Adapted from Williams, G. 1969; p. 125: Figure originally proposed by Ortiz & Zambrano; p. 142: Adapted from image modified by Moreiras, S. and Mastrantonio, L. 2013; pp. 133, 139, 144, 152, 160: Pablo Virgillito; pp. Ramiro Pérez Valenzuela; pp.129, 149: Image modified from Pérez Valenzuela, et al. 2012; pp. 36, 101: Adapted from Wine Folly.com.; p. 105: Developed from Morgan, et al. 2017; Salomon, et al. 2013; Zarraonaindia, et al. 2015); pp. 114, 115; 106, 132, 138, 145, 153, 161: Pablo Ayala.